ERROR
IN THE
TUNNELS

A light at the end of the tunnel is what we all hope
for – as seen here in Sapperton Tunnel.
(Courtesy of Howard Beard, Chair of the
Stroud Local History Society)

TERROR
IN THE
TUNNELS

BRITAIN'S DANGEROUS
RAILWAY HISTORY

ROSA MATHESON

The
History
Press

This book is dedicated to the railway navvies who built the railways that led to the civilisation we have today, and to all local interest and history groups and societies throughout the land because without their passion and commitment so much history, culture and knowledge would be lost.

Cover i
Front,
'unkn
of hor
Welwy

great
place
ent in

Back: 1
now a
and u
(Cour

ere is
nnels
ways.

First published 2017

The History Press
The Mill, Brimscombe Port
Stroud, Gloucestershire, GL5 2QG
www.thehistorypress.co.uk

British Library Cataloguing in Publication Data.
A catalogue record for this book is available from the British Library.

ISBN 978 0 7509 6996 3

Typesetting and origination by The History Press
Printed and bound by CPI Group (UK) Ltd

CONTENTS

ACKNOWLEDGEMENTS

There were many interesting 'finds' in researching this book – and not just the material; the helpful people were such a bonus. With so many tunnels researched there was always someone with a passion for it and I thank them for keeping the story alive in the many ways they do – societies, groups, blogs, websites, campaigns.

For all those interested in tunnels, especially railway tunnels, there is a treasure trove of a website – www.forgottenrelics. co.uk/tunnels – where one can not only find out about historical and current information regarding tunnels, but also about action and interest groups in respect of tunnels. Thanks to Graeme Bickerdike, tunnel historian and site editor, for use of material and helpful pointers. Much appreciated.

Many thanks to all at the 'tunnels':

Clayton
Very warm appreciation to David Porter for his time and patience, comments and great graphics.

Box
Alan Payne of a great local history group (www. boxpeopleandplaces.co.uk) offered enthusiastic support, interest and helpful material as well as an introduction to another invaluable contact, David John Pollard, who provided photographs and text. Also thanks to Doreen Lindegard from Bristol Family History Society for use of her very useful research

.

Bramhope
Help comes from many unexpected quarters and one such was Carl Andrews of 'Soul Architects – Spirit and Place' based in Nottinghamshire.

The two Margarets of Otley Museum and Archive – both were helpful above and beyond the call of duty, such is their passion for their subject.

Stanley Merridrew, president of Wharfedale Family History Group, and fellow member Graham Firth were quick and resourceful in their response, providing very helpful material.

Northchurch
To 'old friend' Chris Heaven for swift action and lovely graphics.

Severn
To long-time supporter and friend Jack Hayward for generously sharing his research, writings and private collection with me.

Sapperton
To Howard Beard, chair of the Stroud Local History Society, for useful photographs.

Queensbury
To the Save Queensbury Tunnel Group whose mission is to reclaim Queensbury Tunnel because 'the tunnel is an asset, not a liability ... it could and should serve a future purpose as a transport link, echoing its intended role'. They ask the question: 'If we can celebrate and protect a pile of stones that used to be a castle, why are we content to turn our backs on great civil-engineering feats and allow dereliction to take hold?' Please lend your support to this worthwhile campaign.

Also, many thanks to:

Phill Davison for use of his amazing tunnel photographs. Phill's interest in and passion for old railway lines has served as an inspiration for others. Check out his 'Secret Leeds 2' and the Gildersome Tunnel story on Facebook – fascinating.

Rog Frost, curator at the lovely Market Lavington Museum, for taking the time to send wonderful pictures from their Alf Burgess Photographic Collection showing real-life navvies at work. Do visit their website and blog, it is a treasure – www.marketlavingtonmuseum.org.uk.

Linda Rollit of Berkhamsted Local History and Museum Society for immediately sending out a call to arms and providing newspaper clippings. 'Picture the Past', image no. PTPD003790 (men at Cowburn Tunnel), is reproduced courtesy of their not-for-profit project that makes historic images from the library and museum collections of Derby, Derbyshire, Nottingham and Nottinghamshire freely available at the click of a button to anyone with access to the Internet, anywhere in the world. You can see over 100,000 pictures at www.picturethepast.org.uk – truly brilliant.

To anyone who has been unacknowledged for help given or for use of photographs and graphics; I hope you will believe it was a genuine oversight or inablility to track them, and that I truly appreciate the help and support given.

As always, thanks to my editor, Amy Rigg, for her calm support, and to my wonderful family who are at the centre of all I do.

INTRODUCTION

TUNNEL – a noun and a verb depending on the word
in front of it: a tunnel; to tunnel.

Tunnels create a frisson of excitement. Tunnelling and entering
a tunnel captures the dark side of the imagination, even in
this modern age. It suggests a journey into the unknown, one
that is fraught with hidden and potential dangers. In 1854,
after a tunnel collapse, *The Spectator* posed the question, 'How
do we know that all tunnels are not in a gradual process of
disintegration?', implying that maybe all tunnels, especially
railway tunnels, were *always* in this process, and, therefore,
always vulnerable. Tunnels have a metaphysical significance –
an enveloping darkness followed, hopefully, and eventually, by
light. Hence the well-used saying 'there is light at the end of
the tunnel'.

To tunnel is to make a tunnel – to tunnel *through* or under
something, usually to get to the other side – but one can also
tunnel *into* something. Man has been creating tunnels over
many thousands of years, for many reasons: to get at what is
inside the earth; to hide in; to get from one place to another;
to wage war. Cavemen created tunnels into the hills to make
caves for dwellings; on Easter Island challenging tunnels led to
spaces of religious significance; captives in times of war tunnel
to escape; whilst others dig tunnels for sanctuary. (In the 1840s
a well-known and wanted chartist, Joseph B. Anderson, spent

'three weeks in the under-ground construction of Bramhope Tunnel, his food being daily supplied to him by his friends'.[1]) There are those who tunnel for profit, and then there are some who tunnel for fun.

Today, tunnelling is a big industry – a specialist industry. There are magazines and associations all about tunnelling. There are even videos on 'how to make your own tunnel'! What then, you may ask, is a tunnel? The definition of what constitutes a tunnel can vary widely from source to source, country to country. The *Oxford English Dictionary* offers the following definition: 'An artificial underground passage, especially one built through a hill, mountain or under a building, road, or river.' A tunnel may be for foot or vehicular road traffic, for rail traffic, or for a canal. The following explanation is from The British Tunnelling Society's website:

> There are many reasons why tunnels or other underground excavations are required, and many methods for their construction. What they all have in common is the need to provide a conduit or space under or through an obstacle, be it a mass transit system under a busy city centre, a high-speed rail line underneath a mountain range or sea, a road link underneath a river, an oil, gas or electricity pipeline, or a water supply or sewer tunnel for a city. The method employed for the construction of a tunnel depends on the length and size, but most importantly on the ground and groundwater conditions through which the tunnel is built.

In planning a tunnel it was necessary to know the geology, and particularly the characteristics, of the different types of rock, clay and sand the tunnel would pass through, and to lay out the line of the tunnel accurately. From that, if necessary, a series of exploratory shafts would be sunk along the line of the tunnel to establish the geology. The information gained would form the basis of the contracts and tenders to dig the tunnel. The exploratory shafts at this stage could be enlarged into working

SECTIONAL VIEW OF THE EXCAVATIONS FOR THE SEVERN TUNNEL, SHOWING THE HARD
AND FOSSILIFEROUS NATURE OF THE GROUND TO BE PENETRATED

As tunnels are essentially holes, the simplest and easiest way to go about making one was to start digging a hole, and keep digging until one got out the other side of where one wanted to come out. This Heath Robinson cartoon of the Severn Tunnel shows it delightfully. (Author's) shafts for taking out the material the tunnel was dug through, and for taking in materials such as timber for centres, bricks, mortar and also for pumping out water if it became a problem. The working shafts could be retained as airshafts.

The resident engineer and his assistants would monitor progress, or lack of it, and report to the chief engineer. If the engineer was satisfied he would sign the certificates and the contractor could draw his payment from the company's bank. At the end of it all there would be a massive clearing-out sale of materials, horses and sundries.[2]

Tunnels were always the hardest part of railway creation, and so were not undertaken lightly. For the railways a tunnel was dug because it was the only, or cheapest, solution to a problem – the problem usually being a hill, a mountain, river, a metropolis or, as quite often happened, an irate landowner who did not want his view 'despoiled' by a smoking monster pulling a trainload of the common people! Edgar Schieldrop elegantly sums up the problem of trying to get a railway line over hills and mountains:

> However clever and ingenious one may be in twisting and turning a railway line through a rising valley, there usually comes a time, sooner or later, when all ways are stopped and one has to decide to tunnel through instead of going over the top. The railway is a very poor climber, even in the hands of the most resourceful engineer.[3]

The cleverness and ingenuity of those early resourceful engineers was severely tested in railway developments, particularly in creating tunnels, but what they created was often awe inspiring. These are the words of James Drake as he travelled on the London and Birmingham Railway line:

> Whilst contemplating modern works of such astonishing magnitude as this, we cannot avoid instituting a comparison between them and the lauded monuments of antiquity;

and much as the cyclopean structures of the ancient world have ben admired and extolled, we think they are equalled, if not surpassed, by many of the stupendous works which have lately been completed in our own country. The railway along which we are travelling is, doubtless, as great a work as the pyramids of Egypt' and the tunnel through we are passing [Grand Kilsby Tunnel] is just about the same length [2,938 yards (1.4 miles or 2.2km)] as the passage which Xerxes cut through Mount Athos and which occupied his army for three years.[4]

Many of these tunnels, particularly their portals and even their shafts, which were iconic then, remain iconic now. Just think of Box, Bramhope, Primrose Hill, Clayton and Kilsby, to name a few, they all shout, 'Look at me!' Happily we too have come to appreciate their cultural worth. Two of the large ventilation shafts, some 60ft (18.29m) in diameter, of the Grand Kilsby Tunnel (designed by Robert Stephenson, supervising engineer for the line) were given a Grade II★ listing by English Heritage in 1987. Nowadays we may wonder at the Victorian taste for decorating, perhaps over-decorating, something of utilitarian use such as a railway. Such finessing, however, tells us a lot about the Victorian's attitudes towards their railways and tunnels, an attitude that reflects their aspirations and ambitions for the nation as a whole.

Tunnels come in different types, sizes and lengths (as well as varying degrees of unpleasantness). An article published in *The Spectator* (30 September 1854) gave a description, as explained to them by 'an engineer':

Tunnels are of various kinds; some cut through solid rock and needing no lining, some through broken masses, some sand and gravel, and some clay; and in addition to this, some are wet and some are dry. When not solid rock, the tunnels are lined with arches of brick or of stone, some set in cement and some in common mortar. If the foundations were perfectly secure against sinking, rapidly hardening cement would be best. In other cases, mortar which sets slowly is best. The foundations of the arch are usually an inverted curve of brick or stone, on which is laid ballast, on the ballast the sleepers' and on the sleepers the rails.

From their very beginnings people developed a curiosity, even a fascination, for railways and their tunnels. The railway companies were very pleased to benefit from this attraction and for a small sum laid on guided tours, which were eagerly taken up by those brave, or foolhardy, enough to chance it. The first report of such can be found in the *Lancaster Gazette*, 30 June 1827:

LIVERPOOL AND MANCHESTER RAIL-ROAD – THE EDGEHILL TUNNEL

The extraordinary and stupendous undertaking of excavating a wide and lofty tunnel, from the shores of the Mersey, under the town, to the other side of Edge Hill, for the passage of carriages to the line of the open railway, is proceeding with as much celerity as the nature of the work will permit. The excavating began at different points on the line of the intended tunnel, the principal 'eyes' being one in White Street, one in Duke Street and one in Mosslake-fields …They are all provided with the usual mining machinery for the hoisting up of the loose material, and the tunnel being driven east and west from each eye, the miners will meet each other in the middle.

The visitor may descend 'the eye' in one of the buckets, with perfect security, and it is a novel and interesting sight to those who have never seen mining in its grander operation to take a view of the noisy operations going on below, the echo of which is confined to the subterranean passage. Though numerous candles are burnt by the workmen, the darkness of the cavern is barely dispersed; the sound of the busy hammer, chisel and pick-axe, the rumbling of the loaded wagons along the railway leading to the further ends of the cavern to the pit, and the frequent blasting of rock, mingling with the hoarse-sounding voices of the miners, whose sombre figures are scarcely visible, form an interesting ensemble of human daring, industry and ingenuity.

It is not only incredible that such a dangerous practice – blasting, with the men still in the tunnel – happened regularly, but also that they were happy to invite visitors into such a situation. Such working conditions would, and inevitably did, lead to accidents – many of them life changing, others fatal. Perhaps the public would have been less enthusiastic about travelling up and down in a bucket having read the following report in a newspaper published a short time after:

Shocking accident:
At 8pm on Wednesday evening, as a party of six men were ascending in the bucket from the railroad shaft in Pitt Street, the horse which was drawing them up having been irritated by some idle boys, proceeded too far, and one man, named ARTHUR M'CONVIL, was caught between the wheel and the rope attached to the bucket, and was terribly crushed about the neck and chest before he could be extricated. M.G. LAMONBY, the surgeon, happened to be looking at the shaft at the time assisted in extricating the poor man, and immediately examined and bled him, and afterwards accompanied him to the Infirmary, where he now lies with little hope of recovery.[5]

Britain holds many 'records' with regard to railway tunnels that were created to surmount all different kinds of problems:

The first tunnel
Archaeologists in Derbyshire have found what they believe is the world's oldest railway tunnel. The tunnel lies on the route of

the Butterley Gangroad, a horse-operated railway built in 1793 to link the Cromford Canal with limestone quarries at Crich.[6]

The first purpose-built railway tunnel and station
Crown Street Station, Liverpool, 1827, was built by George Stephenson. A single-track tunnel 873ft long (266m) was bored by 300 miners/navvies from Edge Hill to Crown Street to serve the world's first intercity passenger railway terminus station.[7]

The oldest used tunnel in the world
The 0.68 miles (1.1km) 1842 Prince of Wales Tunnel, in Shildon near Darlington, England, is the oldest sizeable tunnel in the world still in use under a settlement.[8]

First under water
The Thames Tunnel, built by Marc Isambard Brunel and his son Isambard Kingdom Brunel and opened in 1843, was the first underwater tunnel and the first to be built using a tunnelling shield. Although technically not built as a railway tunnel – it was originally used as a pedestrian tunnel – it was converted to a railway tunnel in 1869.[9]

First under a metropolis
The 2.08 miles (3.34km) Victoria Tunnel/Waterloo Tunnel in Liverpool was bored under a metropolis and opened in 1848. The tunnel was initially used only for rail freight and, later, freight and passengers serving the Liverpool ship-liner terminal. The tunnel's route is from Edge Hill in the east of the city to the north end at Liverpool docks.[10]

First deep-level underground railway
The Mersey Railway Tunnel opened in 1886, running from Liverpool to Birkenhead under the River Mersey. By 1892 the extensions on land from Birkenhead Park Station to Liverpool Central Low Level Station produced a tunnel 3.12 miles (5.02km) in length.[11]

Longest underwater tunnel

The rail Severn Tunnel was opened in late 1886. It is 4.355 miles (7.008km) long, although only 2.2 miles (3.62km) of the tunnel is actually under the River Severn. The tunnel replaced the Mersey Railway Tunnel's longest underwater record.[12]

Happily, a record that Britain does not hold is that of the largest number of deaths at one time caused by an accident in a railway tunnel. That belongs to Italy. On 2 March 1944 a freight train stalled over wet rails on a steep gradient in the Armi Tunnel near Salerno in southern Italy and around

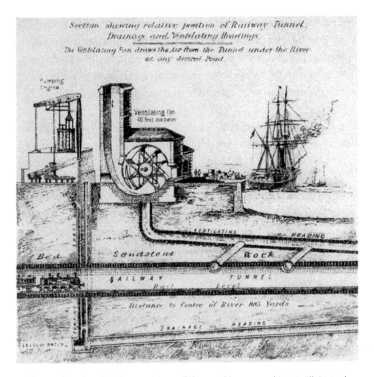

An illustration showing the workings of the machinery used to ventilate and drain the Mersey Railway Tunnel when it first opened in January 1886. Some undertaking! (Mersey Railway Company – PortCities Liverpool, public domain)

520 people – illegal passengers (it was a freight *not* passenger train) and crew – were slowly overcome by carbon monoxide poisoning and died.

Little wonder then that in the early days of railways there was a real fear of tunnels, not only by passengers but also by society at large. Not only did they fear what could happen in them – 'being mashed into a pummy', to quote Charles G. Harper, the social commentator – but they were also concerned about what lasting effects they might have when one eventually came out. The papers carried many 'letters of concern' and editorial pieces on the subject, such as this one published in the *London Evening Standard* on Tuesday 7 March 1837:

> Observations have been made by eminent medical men upon the effect that tunnels produce upon the human frame. The question is an important one, not only to those who are engaged in the construction of railways, but also to the public who are eventually to travel by them.

Drs Paris and Watson who visited the tunnel in progress under Primrose Hill in February 1837 came to the conclusion that:

> The dangers incurred when passing through a well-constructed tunnel are no greater than those incurred when travelling upon an open railway … and the apprehension which has been expressed that such tunnels are likely to prove detrimental to the health or inconvenient to the feelings of those who go through them are perfectly futile and groundless.

The first description of the first ever passenger ride in a railway tunnel (soon to be the Liverpool & Manchester Railway) was written up in *The Lancaster Gazette*, August 1829:

> On Friday, the grand railway tunnel, that runs under the town of Liverpool, from the back of Edge-hill to Wapping,

was opened for the inspection of the public ... Soon after
two the Mayor and his friends, including several of the
proprietors, took their place in a common railway waggon,
fitted with seats for the occasion (the handsome machines
intended for passengers not being yet finished), and being
pushed to the mouth of the great tunnel, set off, down the
gently-inclined plane, without horse or other drag, at a
rapid rate, under the guidance of Mr Harding and his son,
who regulated the speed of the machine by friction lever.
The velocity of the machines was frequently stayed as it
proceeded down this apparently interminable cavern, to
prevent accidents on the passing crowds who walked up and
down the roadway. This precaution, however, was scarcely
thought necessary, for the thunder of the wheels was heard

This beautiful, romanticised drawing is from the series *Coloured Views on
the Liverpool and Manchester Railway* (1833 revised edition) by T.T. Bury.
The inside of Wapping Tunnel, connecting the Liverpool and Manchester
Railway with Wapping Dock in Liverpool, as it was in the 1830s, would bear no
resemblance to the actual reality of the tunnel. (Stapleton Collection, via the
Bridgeman Art Library, public domain)

from one end of the tunnel to the other ... after a delightful ride of about eight to ten minutes, the road taking a slight turn, brought the company again to daylight at the entrance of the tunnel near to Wapping.

A decade later, once rail travel had been established, James Drake, in his book *Drake's Road Book of the London and Birmingham Railway* (1839), gives a highly entertaining and atmospheric description of the experience of riding on the early trains behind a steam engine, through an early tunnel:

> If, however, the traveller prefers keeping his seat and closing the windows which is certainly the most advisable plan [as opposed to hanging out of the window and looking around], he will find himself suddenly, and without a moment's warning, plunged into worse than Cimmerian darkness,[13] and hurried along through clouds of smoke and vapour; amid flying sparks, jarring atoms, rushing winds, and every sign of elemental strife; whilst stunning sounds, an a rattling, clashing din, form a hubbub, than which what Satan heard in his flight through the realms of Chaos and Old Night, could scarcely be more horrific. But let not the most timid traveller imagine that there is any real danger, although appearances are rather alarming, and the consideration that fifty feet of earth are suspended above, is somewhat startling, yet if he would close his eyes for the space of a minute, at the end of that period, he will find himself, like many thousands who have daily preceded before him, safely restored to the pure air and the light of day.[14]

One could not call it an encouraging piece. *The Railway Traveller's Handy Book*, on the other hand, gives helpful hints in how to act on train journeys, from purchasing one's tickets to how to act if one is unfortunate enough to encounter an accident. It is, in typical British fashion, wonderfully understated. Above all, it says one needs 'coolness and judgement'. It advises, 'When the train comes to a sudden standstill, at an unexpected stopping-place, it is usually a sign there is something amiss; but this something may be of very trivial moment.' Should one actually be involved in an accident it suggests: 'If a person be buried among the *debris* of the carriages, and still in possession of life and limb, one should endeavour to make his way out of the perilous position, in an upward direction, and if the windows be blocked up, force a passage in the best manner he can by the aid of a stick or umbrella.' (All very good if one is a man, but what advice for the women?) For an accident in a tunnel it recommends 'a person should grope his way along by the

The disused Miley Tunnel shows clearly the four-foot way (which was often less, i.e. three-foot something) between wall and outside rail that was the 'safe' passage for platelayers and other workmen inside the tunnel. The six-foot way lay between the two inside rails and was an extremely dangerous place to have to lie down in. (Courtesy of Phill Davison)

side of the wall, feeling with his hands, and keeping his body as close to the brickwork as possible'.[15] Getting out and staying close to the wall was very sound advice! The gap between the tunnel wall and the outside rail was known as 'the four foot' and the gap between each set of rails was 'the six foot'; both gaps played significant roles in accidents in tunnels.

Years later, the health debate was still on going, especially as the tunnels grew longer and more ambitious. The making of Box Tunnel in the 1840s drew many gloomy predictions, foretelling that passengers would suffocate whilst travelling through its terrifyingly long length – almost 3,168 yards (1.83 miles or 2.9km). The debate centred on the travelling public – paying people who would be whipped in and out as speedily and as comfortably as possible before they were suffocated or lost their sense! No one appeared to be concerned for the hundreds of thousands of navvies as they picked, shovelled, blasted and bored their way in almost total darkness (apart from the flickering of their candles) through dank earth, treacherous rock and shifting shale, often ankle-deep, or knee-deep, in wet mud in malodorous atmospheres, inhaling obnoxious gases, working in claustrophobic and dangerous conditions, fearing for life and limb – not just for minutes but for days, weeks and even months on end.

Navigators – 'Navvies'
Navigators – or navvies, as they were known – came into being with the building of the canals. The railway navvies became a distinct group because of the nature of their work, but they were not just a class, they were a special kind of community too. Social observers of the time noted the workforce consisted of three types of labourers: 'labourers from the local district who were out of work; wandering labourers, often from Ireland; and a permanent group of labourers who had been employed in building the canals and railways for years.'[16]

With the development of the railways their numbers grew enormously, as did their big, bad reputation. The arrival of these men, and their women and followers, would create panic in villages and even towns. 'The dread which such men as these spread throughout a rural community, was striking, nor was it without cause.'[17] Their anti-social behaviour crossed the whole spectrum of life, so much so they were often viewed as degenerates by polite Victorian society. They lived by their own set of rules, flouting normal conventions such as marriage and paternal responsibility; their habitations were squalid (not always their fault); they ate and drank copious amounts until their wages ran out; they challenged the law, breaking it frequently and also breaking out of prisons. There was also a great deal of licentiousness, a great deal of drunkenness, a great deal of crime and a great deal of fighting, lots of fighting.

H.J. Brown recollects one such altercation when he worked as a young lad at Watford Tunnel:

> To decide this, a fair rough-and-tumble fight, with some nice purring, was proposed among their comrades, and

'On the tramp' is the navvy term for job-hunting. Here a navvy is depicted carrying all his gear on his person, tramping from one job to the next. The cartoon encapsulates people's romanticised version of the real thing. (Private collection)

Navvies are always associated with pick and shovel – the tools of their trade
– but unlike the building of earlier railway lines, by the late 1880s, when this
photograph was taken, mechanical help was available in the shape of the
huge steam 'navvy' seen here being used to dig out the bulk of the cutting.
(Courtesy of Market Lavington Museum)

instantly agreed to. 'Send for the purring-boots!' was the
cry; and the men jumped down from the scaffold, and
repaired to the adjacent field. The purring-boots duly came.
They were stout high-lows, each shod with an iron-plate,
standing an inch or so in advance of the toe. Each man was
to wear one boot, with which he was to kick the other
to the utmost. A toss took place for right or left, and the
winner of the right having a small foot the boot was stuffed
with hay to make it fit. I refrain from particulars: I have
said enough to show the brutal nature of the affray. It lasted
more than an hour. The victor was a pitiable object for
months, and his foe was crippled for life. Here I must add,

This photograph is part of the Alf Burgess Photograph Collection from the Market Lavington Museum. Burgess set up his commercial photographic studio in Market Lavington in 1886 but also made it his business to record local goings on, including the Great Western Railway route-shortening line which passed through the parish, making Lavington a railway station on what was to become the new main line between London, Exeter, Plymouth and Penzance. Here we see some of the navvies posing for Mr Burgess. He must have made a welcome diversion for them – it was so much easier to pose than to dig the cutting through the Parham Wood area. These chaps do not suggest the outrageous, colourful navvies one knows of. By this time, however, the navvies had become an institution and their behaviour and habits had calmed a great deal. (Courtesy of Market Lavington Museum)

that the old fashion of deciding questions by the trial of combat prevailed widely among the first race of navvies.[18]

Undoubtedly the railway navvy was a colourful character, but there was another important facet to him, often conveniently overlooked: he was essential to the building of the railways. Baldly stated, without him the work could not have been done. John Francis wrote in 1851:

rare and in Bune by J C Bourne

INTERIOR OF BOX TUNNEL

The making of Box Tunnel had an horrendously high death toll. It is said at least 100 navvies lost their lives. (Drawing taken from railway artist J.C. Bourne's book *Great Western Railway*, private collection)

he is an important portion of this new system of political economy. He risks life and limb to form the works which we admire. He braves all weathers, he dares all danger, he labours with a power and purpose which demand attention. Whilst others, 'the great men', conceived, designed and invented, the navvy got his hands dirty and did the 'hard graft' to deliver their dreams.

It is well to remember that without the navvy, and the railways they built, we would not have the civilization that we have today, and we should therefore give the navvy – the master builder – his due.

The public had little idea of the circumstances these men laboured in, but a graphic description in the *Taunton Courier and Western Advertiser* (which was writing very 'kindly' about their experience and the contractors) regarding working in Box Tunnel gives some idea of what it was like:

In its present unfinished state it is not attractive ... There was a want of free circulation of air and the smell and smoke of gunpowder. The dark, dim vault filled with vapour, is saved from utter and black darkness by the feeble light of candles, which are stuck upon the sides of the excavation, and placed on trucks, or other things used in the carrying on of the works; those which are in your immediate neighbourhood omit a dull red light, are seen gradually diminishing in seize and effect, till they appear like small red dots, and are then lost in the dark void. Taking a candle in your hand you pick your way through pools of water, over the temporary rails, among blocks of stone and the huge chains attached to the machinery which every now and then impede your way ... stepping sometimes on solid rock and others loose fragments or stones, you wind your way slowly and with difficulty ...

Presently your attention is excited by a strange light, before you the perfect darkness is broken by a faint grey streak, which at first scarcely perceptible soon assumes a stronger hue: you proceed til you find yourself and your companions standing under an opening from above in an uncertain and unearthly light looking like 'lated ghosts' ...

Not during all this time have your ears been idle, the sounds of the pick, the shovel and the hammer have fallen upon them indistinctly … having been informed that a 'shot' is to be fired at the further extremity you stop to listen and judge the effects. The match is applied, the explosion follows and a concussion such as you probably have never felt before, takes place, the solid rock appears to shake, and the reverberation of the shock and sound is sensibly and fearfully experienced.

Unsurprisingly then, with the coming of the railways and the 'Railway Age', there also came the coming of the railway accident – especially in tunnels. Not for nothing did people fear them. Accidents in tunnels came in many hideous, horrifying forms:

A Litany of Terror

Explosions	blown to pieces
Collapses	buried alive
Flooding	drowned
Trapped	asphyxiation
Falls	crushed to death

All of these possibilities were realities *before* the railway was even completed. Then, when it was, there was the possibility of:

Collisions	battered to death / scalded to death / smothered / decapitation / broken to bits
Fire	burned alive
Accident	mown down by a train

All gruesome possibilities. On top of all that there is the grief. Grief for lives lost and grief for lives damaged or irreparably changed. So, take a deep breath before you continue reading …

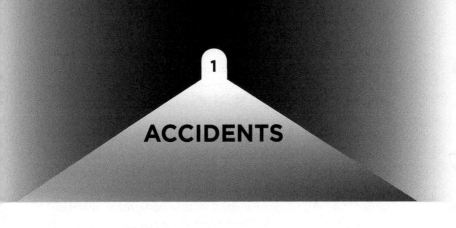

ACCIDENTS

Accidents during the making of tunnels resulted from many kinds of happenings – things falling down from shafts or tunnel roofs; being hit by/or hitting one's self with the equipment; people falling over, falling down or tripping up; things filling up with water; things blowing up and things being blown down! They came about from poor or faulty equipment; inattention; risk-taking; being in the wrong place at the wrong time; bad luck; dreadful conditions; ill health and exhaustion. At the forefront of those who paid the price was the railway navvy.

Box Tunnel – Just How Many Lost Their Lives?

Box Tunnel was, and continues to be, a masterpiece of engineering. The *Salisbury and Winchester Journal* (July 1841) called it: 'One of the most wonderful specimens of the skill and perseverance of our countrymen which the world presents.' Box Hill, in which the tunnel lies, was also a wonderful specimen, a formidable physical barrier that needed to be overcome to complete the Great Western Railway's main-line section between Bath and Swindon. There were several challenges to delivering what is, undoubtedly, now seen as one of Brunel's iconic achievements. It was a work of monumental difficulties;

Thomas Gale, foreman who worked on the construction of the tunnel, describes them as 'appalling difficulties' in a day when such engineering feats were accomplished by the muscle power of man and horse, with the blows of picks and hammers and the blasts of gunpowder.

Work started in September 1836, under the charge of William Glennie, one of Brunel's personal assistants, with the sinking of six permanent shafts and two temporary ones. When completed the shafts measured 28ft (8.5m) in diameter and the deepest was 290ft (88m). All workmen, construction equipment, materials and 247,000 cubic yards (189,000m³) of extract had to go in and come out of these shafts. The shafts also functioned as the safety exits from the tunnel, especially necessary as, due to the time period required to get men in and out of the workings, blasting occurred with the men inside the tunnel. Once completed, shafts No. 1 (western end) and No. 8 (eastern end) had been enlarged into openings to form the entrance to the tunnel.

In February 1837 notices for tenders were issued for the contract of Box Tunnel, stipulating that the excavation work had to be completed within thirty months – by August 1840. Two local teams – William Jones Brewer, a quarry master from Box, and Thomas Lewis, a builder from Bath – gained one of the contracts. They started excavation from the difficult eastern end – one at each end of their section working and blasting towards the other. There was great excitement and anticipation about whether their two ends would meet. They did. They met with just a hair's breadth, a mere 5cm between them, much to the delight of Brunel who was present at the completing moment. In fact, the tunnel is completely straight – a true engineering achievement.

George Burge, of Herne Bay, some distance hence, but a man with a big reputation, having worked with Thomas Telford, was given the contracts for the western end. For his navvies it was a matter of sweat, picks and shovels. There was a tight schedule to meet and so work was continuous, twenty-four hours a day, with one shift relieving the other. Candles provided the only

BOX TUNNEL STONE QUARRIES.

We are obliged for your order which is having our attention.
Yours faithfully,   YOCKNEY & Co.

The lesser-known Box Tunnel, East Mouth. This spot was known to the older folk locally as Kites Nest. A fall of stone from the roof of the tunnel in 1897 led to the building of a brick arch within the tunnel to protect the line from further falls. This was possible due to the generous structure gauge on former broad-gauge lines; however, in 2015 it was necessary to lower the track under the arch to provide clearance for the rigid overhead conductor rail system to be installed for the new electric trains.

The smaller tunnel on the right dates from *c.* 1844. It led to an underground loading wharf in Corsham Down Quarry. The quarry was converted into the Central Ammunition Depot between 1937 and 1940; the quarry tunnel was enlarged, however, it was still too small for main-line locomotives. (Text and photograph courtesy of David John Pollard)

lighting as they toiled in the darkness and were consumed at the rate of 1 ton per week, equalled by the weekly consumption of explosives. Over 30 million bricks were used, although not the entire tunnel was lined with them. After numerous setbacks it was eventually opened on 30 June 1841, although the men still continued to build the fine-looking west portal.

This amazing endeavour was achieved on the backs, health and lives of working men – the railway navvies. The many detractors at the time who foresaw only calamity with the tunnel were thinking of the train travellers, but for the poor navvy who constructed this magnificent piece of Brunel ambition, they were often proved right. The tunnel was not only expensive in terms of resources but also expensive in terms of lives. Commenting on this sad situation in June 1839 the *South Eastern Gazette* remarked, 'The consumption of human life at this enormous undertaking has been has been frightful,' and by that point it was yet to be finished. Thanks to the local press we have an insight in to the number and type of accidents that occurred:

1838
Wiltshire Independent, Thursday 27 September
On Saturday morning last as Daniel THOMAS, a native of Wick Hill near Bremhill, was working at the top of Shaft No 5, he fell from the woodwork to the bottom … and but for a quantity of water at the bottom of the shaft, he would in all probability have been dashed to pieces. He was taken up alive but survived only a few hours. A Coroner's Inquest was held on the body the next day – Verdict: *Accidental Death*.

Canterbury Journal, Kentish Times and Farmer's Gazette, Saturday 20 October
19 persons have already been killed in accidents.

Wiltshire Independent, Thursday 22 November
On the night of Friday last, as one of the bricklayers employed at Shaft No 5 … walking near the mouth of the shaft, the night being so dark, he unfortunately stepped into the pit, to the bottom of which he fell, some 290 feet. His head was dashed to pieces and his bones broken in the most dreadful manner. It appears the man was quite sober when the accident happened. This is the 20th life lost on the works of Box Tunnel.

1839 Blasting Accidents

Devizes and Wiltshire Gazzette, Thursday 28 February

An Inquest was held on Friday on the body of Charles Biggins, aged 21, who came by his death the previous day in consequence of injuries received at No 2 pit box. The deceased with others was engaged in blasting. During an explosion the deceased unfortunately placed himself in a place that was dangerous and received the injuries which caused his death, he was promptly attended by a medical gentleman, but died within six hours. The Jury being satisfied that no blame was attached to any person. Verdict: *Accidental Death.*

Wiltshire Independent, Thursday 11 July

On Saturday last another shocking accident happened at Shaft No 4, to a man named FALKIN, who was blasting the rock. It appears the poor fellow, not being aware the match was slighted, advanced to near when suddenly the mine exploded and the stones cut his head dreadfully. He is now laying in a dreadful state and little or no hope is entertained of him.

Taunton Courier and Western Advertiser, Wednesday 31 July

The preservation of life under circumstances of the gravest danger has sometimes been almost miraculous, as the following anecdote will show: A few weeks ago a man was about to 'fire-a-shot' that is to blow up a piece of rock. He had prepared the hole for the charge, and was in the act of pouring gunpowder into it from an iron cannister, containing about twenty pounds, which he held under his arm, when a drop of water having fallen from the roof upon the wick of his candle, most imprudently placed close to the hole, a spark flew from it into the powder causing the most horrific explosion. The cannister was burnt to atoms, but

Navvies at work on Cowburn Tunnel, c. 1891, about to be lowered into the shaft in a bucket, or 'skiff', or 'skep' (normally a woven basket of wicker or wood) as it was sometimes called. Seeing its precarious nature, it is not surprising that so many accidents occurred because of arrangements such as these. Every tunnel had such a story to tell. 'Winching' changed greatly as more technology became available over nineteenth-century railway building, but accidents still occurred. Despite the late decade, this one looks pretty basic. (Courtesy of Jane Goldsmith and www.picturethepast.org.uk)

not one piece entered the poor unfortunate man who held it; he was dreadfully burned, his clothes were torn off and his hair and eyebrows completely destroyed, and the skin burned off all around his body, but, wonderful to relate, his eyesight was uninjured, and, although from the actions of the flames he was miserably wounded and disfigured, he is now in a fair way of recovery. Some of his fellow workmen who were at a distance of several yards, were knocked down and severely scorched.

1840

Accidents of 'falling down shafts' and 'material falling on men' were common. 1840 was to prove a desperate year, as the men were driven to their limits in order to fulfil the contract's end, now just months away.

Bristol Mirror, 22 February

Friday last, a poor man called Robert PRICE, a native of Bradford, employed above ground at Box Tunnel advanced too far down the mouth of the shaft, 296 feet, and was dashed to pieces.

Bristol Mirror, 29 February

A fatal accident in No. 3 Shaft, Box Tunnel as men were lowering a skiff filled with bricks, the rope broke and the whole fell to the bottom, over 200 feet, killing a man called BAILEY and very much injuring another.

On Wednesday there was another accident when a stone fell on a man called OSBORNE who was coming up No. 5 Shaft when a stone knocked him out of the skiff and he fell to the bottom, breaking his leg and his arm in two places and injuring his head. His arm was amputated at Bath Hospital but there is not the slightest hope of his recovery.

Bristol Mirror, 11 July

Inquest at Box on a man named PICKET whose death was caused by a fall of one of the supports at Box Tunnel.

Bristol Mirror, 18 July

Fatal accident at No. 7 Shaft, Box Tunnel where seven men were at work sinking, the sides of the pit fell in, killing one man at once and another died during the course of a day. Two more were not expected to recover and the other three were seriously injured.

Bristol Mirror, 1 August

On Thursday a young man named SHEPPARD, a native of Atworth, went to the engine house of No. 7 Shaft, Box Tunnel (it is believed in a state of intoxication) and went to sleep. In his slumbers he rolled under a beam which came down on his head. He was crushed to pieces.

Wiltshire Independent, 7 November

Three men in the last week have lost their lives at the Box Tunnel, in the shaft at Corsham, by material falling on them and two others have mangled limbs.

1841

Bristol Mirror, 17 April

On Saturday evening last a fatal accident occurred near No. 8 Shaft, Box Tunnel. A poor man named STAFFORD of sober and industrious habits was following his work a short distance from where others were blasting when a large stone fell on the head of the poor fellow, which so injured him, he survived only a few hours.

Even after its opening, as the men continued to work, the accidents continued to happen:

Bristol Mirror, 18 September

John BURN, was blasting at Box Tunnel when a down train came out of its regular time; he was njured so severely that he has since died. Another man had both his hands cut off.[1]

Wiltshire Independent, Thursday 5 June 1845

Yesterday morning a mason employed in turning an arch in No. 7 Shaft of the Box Tunnel, unfortunately met with a serious accident by falling from a scaffold 26 feet high. He had finished a portion of his work; and, on turning round to ask the foreman for further instructions, his foot slipped, and he was precipitated to the ground. The unfortunate man sustained a fracture to the right side of the jawbone, broke several of his ribs, and received other serious injuries. He was immediately taken to the United Hospital where his case is considered hopeless. His name is Worthy Guy of Chippenham. He has a wife who has been confined only a fortnight.

The huge loss of life makes for sad reading. Of the 4,000 men who worked there over the five-year construction, it is said some 100 lost their lives, whilst many others were maimed with life-changing injuries or left in a state of ill health from the dreadful conditions. This was to be the story of so many tunnels.

Clayton Tunnel – A Considerable Sensation

Clayton Tunnel of the Great Northern Railway is just a stone's throw from the other tunnel on the line – Queensbury Tunnel (of which more later). This newspaper report is an almost blow-by-blow account of how an accident can happen, and as such it is a incredible insight into what was an everyday working practice for the navvies. The incident which happened at 6 a.m. on Wednesday 4 November 1874 created 'considerable sensation among the navvies on that line',[2] so much so that all work in that shaft was suspended for a number of days – this in a community used to bad accidents as everyday occurrences. There was a great deal of ill ease generated by the accident, as it

Clayton Tunnel's fateful shaft – a long look up and a long fall down. (Courtesy of Phill Davison)

shook the trust that navvies had in the enginemen who raised and lowered them to and from the depths of the pit below.

William Francis Taylor and Edward Keats/Kates (different spellings in different accounts) were the two enginemen involved, and it is obvious that, if it was not due to faulty machinery, it would be a fault of negligence of one or both of these men. They both vehemently denied it was their error, each pointing the finger of blame at the other:

Bradford Observer, Thursday 5 November 1874

On the line of the Great Northern Railway, from Halifax to Bradford, and thence to Thornton, there are two very heavy tunnels in the course of construction, one under Clayton Heights, about 1,000 yards in length, and that under Queensbury, about 2,000 yards long. Along the line of the tunnel first named, four shafts have been sunk so that headings can be driven simultaneously from eight different points, and the works connected with these headings are carried on night and day almost without cessation.

Over the shaft at which the accident occurred, large timber scaffolding, or head gear has been fixed, surmounted by a pulley from four to five feet wide, and by means of this the rubbish from below is raised to the top of the shaft; and at a few yards distant from the mouth of the shaft an engine for winding up the tubs of debris, and pumping water, has been planted.

There are usually eleven men in each shift at the bottom of the shaft, and at six o'clock on Wednesday morning, Henry Hickman, one of the sub-contractors, gave orders for the day shift to go down and relieve the night men, and accordingly four of them got into the tub or cage to descend. Before this could be done, however, it was necessary that the cage should be raised a little, in order that the 'lorry' might be drawn back a little from underneath to allow the skep and the men to descend.

When the lorry was withdrawn, the order was given to lower, but from whatever cause, the engine had not been reversed, and instead of being lowered, the skep was drawn to the top of the head gear and went backwards over the pulley, the result being that one of the men, Thomas Coates, Hickman's brother-in-law, fell to the bottom of the shaft, a depth of 35 yards, was horribly crushed and died in five minutes. The other three men fell to the ground about five yards from the pit mouth, with the skep after them, and were all seriously injured as they had fallen nearly 40 feet. The names of the three men who then so narrowly escaped were William Elliott of Queensbury, whose internal injuries were such as to preclude any hope of recovery, James Spillbury from Shelf, and William Williams. The third was the least injured of any, but still suffered from dislocation of the hip and a few bruises. They were all conveyed as soon as possible to the Infirmary in this town, and arrived there about half-past eight o'clock; and from the first no hope could be held out of Elliott's recovery as he was suffering from a fractured pelvis and other severe internal injuries, while Spillbury had sustained concussion of the brain, and he was then also in great danger, though his recovery was not despaired of.

The body of Coates was removed to the Royal Hotel, Clayton, where on Thursday afternoon an inquest was opened before Mr Barstow, deputy coroner.

The wife of the deceased, Tamar Ann Coates, said that her late husband was twenty-seven years of age, and lived at Clayton Heights. He was working as a filler in the employ of her two brothers, who were sub-contractors under Messrs Benton and Woodiwiss, the contractor for the railway.

Mr John Fawthrop, surgeon, Queensbury, said he had seen the body of the deceased at the Royal Hotel, at about eight o'clock on the morning of the accident, and found beside a lacerated wound on the chin and sundry bruises and scratches, a fracture of both thighs, and concussion of the brain, the latter having caused death.

James Bright, banksman at No.4 shaft on the tunnel, said when the accident occurred he was on the bank top, and saw Coates, Elliott and two other men get into the skep, then resting on the lorry which runs over the mouth of the shaft. Witness gave four signal 'raps' which meant that the engineman was to raise the skep a few feet, in order that the lorry might be drawn from underneath them, and the instructions were obeyed. He then gave two raps, meaning to lower the skep to the bottom of the shaft, but instead of that the skep went right up the pulley on top of the head-gearing, and when he gave one rap to stop the engine, the skep was drawn right over the pulley, and fell on the ground between the shaft and the engine-house. Deceased either jumped or was thrown out, and fell right down the shaft. There were two men in charge of the engine, one of whom worked the day and the other the night shift, namely William Francis Taylor, and Edward Keats, but he could not say which of them was on duty at the time. Keats ought to have been on until six o'clock, and it then wanted a minute or two to six, it being very dark at the time. Witness had heard that a skep had been pulled over on Saturday.

Mark Radford, a miner who was working in the pit at the time, picked up the deceased. He was not dead, but died in a few minutes. Witness brought his body to the top of the shaft.

Henry Hickman, sub-contractor, deposed that he was standing near the pit mouth and saw the accident happen. He heard the raps given to raise the lorry with the four men in it, and it was lifted a few feet and then stopped half a minute, and then it was drawn up to the pulley. Immediately after the accident Taylor ran out of the engine-house and came to the top of the shaft, when he asked witness, 'Oh Harry, who's down the shaft?' and he replied 'Tom Coates.' Then Taylor said again, 'That _____ [meaning Keats] has left a trap for me, he left the engine in motion,' and then Taylor was as white as a sheet. Keats was away half an hour from the time the accident happened.

Wilkinson Andrews, aged seventeen, stoker and cleaner for Taylor, said he was at the engine-house five minutes before the accident happened, and the engine was not then in motion. No one was on the driver's seat at the time, and as it wanted five minutes to the time, he turned round and sat down, and the next he heard was some shouting outside on the bank. Witness then saw the rope coming slack on the drum, and immediately after Jacob Wright cried out, 'You've pulled a poor fellow into the pit.' Taylor, Hoyle and Keats then ran out, and witness stopped the engine which was then running the rope off the drum. He could not tell who set on the engine. All that Taylor had said to witness since the accident was, 'It was cruel of Ned.' Since then, witness had not spoken to Keats.

Henry Hoyle, aged thirteen, stoker for Keats, said that Keats was going to the seat, when Taylor said, 'Come away' and Keats then put some oil on his hands, and was drying them, when the accident occurred. Witness saw Taylor go to the seat as soon as Keats left it, and the engine was then standing, and continued so for fully a minute after Taylor got onto the seat. When Taylor started it, he put full steam on, and must have thought the skep was at the bottom.

George Richardson, a labourer on the line, said he was passing the door of the engine-house about five minutes before the accident happened, and he then saw Taylor on the driver's seat. Witness went into the engine-house some time afterwards, and heard Taylor say that he would take his 'dying oath' that he was not on the seat at all.

No further evidence was then called and the inquiry was left in this unsatisfactory state – involving something like recrimination between the two engine drivers – until next Tuesday when it will be resumed.

We regret to say that while the inquiry, as given above, was going on, the other man (Elliott), most seriously injured, and was laid dead in the Infirmary. The other two men, still at the Infirmary, are progressing towards recovery.[3]

When the court resumed, each engineman accused the other. Keats told the court he was sure it was not him but Taylor 'who drew up the skep when it went over the trolley'. After lowering the skep onto the trolley for the men to get into, he (Keats) 'never meddled with the engine again'. Taylor's story was more involved. He told how he and Keats had:

> compared watches and it wanted five or six minutes until six o'clock [that is, it was still not time for him to take over]. The engine was then standing. He turned away to put his dinner in the cupboard and take his jacket off when heard a signal, but could not say whether it was to pull or to lower. When he turned round again Keats was in the driver's seat.

Then, Taylor said, he told Keats to 'come away' as it was near six o'clock, but before he himself could settle on the driver's seat he heard shouting outside 'and saw the rope on the drum coming slack'. One witness told how Taylor had cried, 'that bugger's done for me.' Taylor told the court that Keats had 'not informed him whether the skep was at the bottom or at the top, as he should have done'. Taylor was an experienced man; he had been an engine driver for twenty-eight years; he should have known what questions he should have asked. Maybe it was this that convinced the jury he was responsible. Twelve of the fourteen jurymen found him 'guilty of manslaughter against William Francis Taylor'.[4]

When there is an accident the question that is always asked is, 'Who is to blame?'
To quote Marcus Aurelis, Roman Emperor AD 161–80: 'We are too much accustomed to attribute to a single cause that which is the product of several, and the majority of our controversies come from that.'[5] It was the responsibility of two separate organisations to determine the who, what, why, when and how of railway accidents, and to disentangle the 'single' and the 'several'. These organisations were the Board of

The grievance is written loud and clear on the tombstone, but the 'person at fault' is not named. (Phill Davison)

Trade's Railway Inspectorate and the coroner and jury in the coroner's court.

The coroner's court

The court is presided over by the coroner who holds an inquiry, or inquest, on the body of the deceased, killed in the accident or, in this discourse, the railway accident. The jury, for this court, like any other jury in the land, is made up from one's peers, who are sworn in and deliver the verdict. They cannot sentence, but can find people guilty and send them to the judicial courts for trial. They can also make recommendations. In the coroner's court, juries were flexible in number, but could not include anyone with any connection or interest in the company being investigated. The jury always visited the scene of the crime to see first-hand where the incident had taken place. They also always viewed the dead wherever they may have been taken.

Whilst health and safety in those times appear to us modern-day readers to be almost non-existent, there were, however, in such dangerous situations, expectations that those in charge should fulfil. These were highlighted in detail by the coroner at the inquest of those who died in the Wickwar Tunnel explosion. It was, he told the jury, his duty to inform them that the law required:

> all parties, whether private individuals or public bodies, carrying on works of the kind in which this accident had originated, and, indeed, all work, should take proper care, use such means as common sense and prudence would dictate, to protect the lives and limbs of her Majesty's subjects employed by them. If it should appear to them that on the present occasion, any individual or individuals, whose duty it was to use such prudent and careful circumspection, had been negligent of his duty, it was in their power and it was their bounden duty, to return a verdict of manslaughter against all such, and send them to their trials before a judge and jury.

When a coroner investigates a death, the public must have access to records that include, among other things, the following:

the location where the body was found and, if different, the location where the death occurred;
the name of the person reporting the death;
the name of the person certifying the death;
date and location of an autopsy;
the name of the person who performed the autopsy;
probable cause, probable manner and probable mechanism of death;
a verdict, and, sometimes, a recommendation.

Coroner's courts at that time were held in many different places, often in local public houses.

Board of Trade Railway Inspectors – HM Railway Inspectorate
The Railway Inspectorate, under the umbrella of the Board of Trade, came into being in 1840 as a result of the Railway Regulations Act (1840). The 'Inspectors' were experienced

Engineers but recruited purely from the military, the Corps of Royal Engineers. Their job was to investigate accidents reported by the railway companies to the Board of Trade, make their findings available to the Coroner's Court, and to submit a report to Parliament. These reports were published and so made available to everyone – including the public.[6]

These men brought a wealth of technical knowledge, experience and a professional integrity to their new detective/ forensic roles, as well as an unbiased and independent view – although the railway companies and the railway press would hotly dispute the latter.

For anyone interested in railway history their reports make fascinating reading, and one can be confident that the facts would be correct. Unlike records and histories written by individuals who had a reputation to protect, or by individual companies proclaiming their achievements, or even by railway fans, all of which are often written in rose-coloured ink, the inspector's reports are written with professional detachment, by people with no axe to grind, but whose job it was to ensure the safety of the travelling public and railway servants.

Bramhope Tunnel – And Mausoleum

The Leeds and Thirsk Railway was the manufacturers' and merchant peoples' of Leeds answer to 'Railway King' George Hudson, when he bought and closed the Leeds & Selby Railway in order to funnel all railway traffic through York. The locals wanted, and needed, a route that allowed them to ferry their raw goods in and their products out more conveniently. Parliamentary approval was sought and gained for their railway in 1845. The route they decided on involved a planned 1¾-mile tunnel at Bramhope, which, when finished, was actually 2 miles and 243 yards long (3.441km) (because

Bramhope Tunnel's Gothic north portal is majestic, a bold statement for the railway company and an impressive entrance to an equally impressive tunnel, which 2.138 miles (3,745 yards) long. Compared to Box Tunnel, the numbers killed here in this equally challenging piece of engineering were remarkably low, although still publicly and grandly acknowledged

the southern end was extended to deal with water problems). It was 25ft 6in wide (7.8m) by 25ft high (7.6m), with a maximum depth in some places of 290ft (88m).

The gradient from Arthington Station to Horaforth Summit is 1 in 94, which played a significant role in an accident in 1854.

Owing to its length and nature, Bramhope Tunnel has an inordinate number of shafts. Work on the first of the planned twelve temporary and four permanent shafts commenced in November 1845, but later a further three were added in order to combat the constant inflow of water, making a grand total of nineteen! What a lot of trouble they all were, as can be seen from the following engineer's reports:

ENGINEER'S REPORT ON PROGRESS

JUNE 1846
A 2ft square culvert
collapsing Shaft 1a Shale.
Water considerable.
(i.e. Horsforth end)
"1b Rock.
"1 Rock. Very little water.
"2 Standing. Waiting for
pumps.
Permanent 3 Lost to water.
Shaft 4 Standing, broken
crank.
"5 Pumping 338 gallons per
minute day and night for two
months without being able
to overcome the spring.
Permanent Drowned out
Shaft 7 Stopped – engine
accident.
"10 Standing – no engine.
Permanent 12 Slip of rock
has been secured, encasing
raised to proper height,
excavating commenced.
Shaft 13 In the tunnel.
"14 Briefly standing,

drowned, larger engine to be
erected.
850 men. 85 horses.

AUGUST 1846
1a wet and heavy. Hard
  white stone.
1 sunk into body of tunnel.
2 22 ft of tunnel – 9 inches
  tunnel
3 25 ft excavated
4 nil
5 water
6 22 ft
7 pumping
8 31 ft
9 22 ½ ft a thin seam of coal
10 water – lack of pump
12 8 ft water disappears into
  rocks
13 17 in the body of tunnel
  373 galls per minute night
  and day
14 going well – 1869 men

It took four long, hard, desperate and dangerous years, from
1845 to 1849, to complete this mammoth piece of work. It was
four years of purgatory for the navvies, who blasted, hewed and
cut the rock, sandstone, shale and clay, coping with the never-
ending enormous volumes of water.

Records show that of the total of 1,869 men employed
there in August 1846 there were 188 quarrymen, 102 masons,

101 labourers, 732 tunnel men, 738 excavators and 18 carpenters. Many of these paid a heavy price with injuries or death. Whilst there were no official accident records kept until 1847, the local papers reported the accidents:

Leeds Times, Saturday 15 August 1846

INQUEST: an inquest was held on the body Gaythorpe Firth, a labourer. The deceased was 19 years of age and had been employed at Bramhope Tunnel ... on Saturday the 25th ult., at shaft No 1 a small stone fell from an ascending bucket, at the height of 70 feet, and struck him on the left temple. He was taken up in a state of insensibility, but later seemed in a fair way for recovery, when he was so imprudent to lie down on the damp ground, in consequence of which, and his refusal to take the medicine supplied to him, a relapse took which terminated fatally on Saturday.
VERDICT: The deceased came by his death from a slight injury ... but that death was accelerated by his own misconduct.

It would appear that in 1847 the number of accidents began to trouble the directors of the company so much so that, in that year, they inaugurated a spring cart service to transport the injured (and the dead) to Leeds General Infirmary and increased their subscription to that institution as well as to The House of Recovery on Beckett Street.[7]

Leeds Times, Saturday 16 October 1847

FATAL ACCIDENT AT BRAMHOPE TUNNEL – YESTERDAY
(Friday) Mr Blackburn, coroner, held an inquest at the Court House upon the body of John Wood, aged 33, employed at Bramhope Tunnel and engaged in attending one of the engines used there. On the 29th ultimo, something becoming wrong with a crank, the deceased mounted the flywheel and his weight caused it to turn round. He was carried round once, and thrown off with such fearful violence that he sustained

a compound fracture of his right thigh and both legs. He was taken to the Infirmary the same day and died there on Wednesday morning.

VERDICT: Accidental death.

Leeds Times, Saturday 7 October 1848

A SERIOUS ACCIDENT

Four men were severely injured in the Bramhope Tunnel ... on Tuesday evening. It appears that a number of workmen were arching a portion of the tunnel near the shaft No 8 when a heavy stone fell from the side of the excavation and drove in the centre, burying eight of them. Three of the four men injured it is believed will recover, but the fourth being severely contused internally, his recovery is doubtful.

The headstone of one of the men who lost his life in the tunnel – James Myers, a miner from Yeadon and buried in Yeadon – is inscribed with the seemingly prophetic words:

What dangers do surround
Poor miners everywhere
And they that labour underground
They should be men of prayer.

There were many of these Bramhope miners to be found in the Otley Parish churchyard, until, as reported in the papers, those killed and already buried there were disinterred and reburied in a special tomb:

Bradford Observer, Thursday 21 June 1849

THE NAVVIES AND THE MAUSOLEUM

... this vast tomb being completed 23 bodies which had previously been deposited in different parts of the churchyard *were disinterred and placed in it*; sufficient space still remaining for many more. This done the tomb was covered in with immense stones laid across ...

The 'tomb' was a memorial to those killed:

Morning Post, Tuesday 19 June 1849
INAUGURATION OF A TOMB
On Sunday evening the parish church of Otley was filled to almost overflowing in consequence of announcement that the large and unique tomb which has been erected in the burial ground adjacent to the church in memory of the thirty-four unfortunate workman who have been killed during the progress of the work in Bramhope Tunnel … would be inaugurated by the performance of a divine service … The tomb or monument is a beautiful work of art of striking interest …

This Mausoleum, representing Bramhope Tunnel itself, and its dedication stone alongside, is a truly amazing memorial to the men who lost their lives in making the tunnel. It shows a respect not generally accorded to navvies at that time. The only other I have come across is a retrospective one in Crookes Cemetery, dedicated by the members of Sheffield Irish Community in 1998 – a small gilt plaque on a rough-cut rock buried in the ground, saying: 'To Commemorate The Unknown Irish Navvies Who Died Building The Totley Tunnel Circa 1880 R.I.P.' (Unfortunately the '0' should have been an '8', as the tunnel was built between 1888–94.) It is believed many of the Totley navvies and their young families died in a smallpox outbreak in 1892. (Courtesy of Otley Council and Museum)

The service was conducted by the Rev. Joshua Hart, the vicar at the time, and the service was 'solemn and impressive'. It included mention of 'a young man having been killed in the tunnel the preceding day'.[8] The local paper carried the folowing report:

Leeds Intelligencer, Saturday 16 June 1849
ANOTHER FATAL ACCIDENT IN THE BRAMHOPE TUNNEL

On Saturday afternoon last, an accident attended with fatal consequences happened to a young man of the name of Cawthrs aged 18, a native of Yeadon, in shaft No. 10 ½ of the above tunnel. The deceased, his brother and two other men were at work in the shaft abovementioned, when the workmen in the next shaft No 10, after giving the usual signals, let off a blast. The deceased and his fellow workers being at a distance of 210 feet from the blast, thought themselves perfectly safe, and continued at their work; but the result showed their mistake, for such was the force of the explosion, that two large stones were thrown even at that distance, and struck the deceased in the face and forehead and smashed it to pieces. He expired almost immediately. His brother had a very narrow escape as the other stone passed close by where he was standing.

The 'tomb' is topped with a large miniature of the mighty north portal of the tunnel with 'exquisite workmanship executed by Mr Francis Lapish and Mr Jonas Clapham of Bradford'. A tombstone that stands by the monument bears the inscription:

**OF THE UNFORTUNATE MEN
WHO LOST THEIR LIVES WHILE ENGAGED IN
THE CONSTRUCTION OF THE
BRAMHOPE TUNNEL OF THE LEEDS AND
THIRSK RAILWAY**

FROM 1845 TO 1949.
THIS TOMB IS ERECTED AS A MEMORIAL
AT THE EXPENSE OF JAMES BRAY, ESQ.,
THE CONTRACTORS AND
THE AGENTS, SUB-CONTRACTORS AND
WORKMEN THEREON

***

I AM A STRANGER AND SOJOURNER WITH YOU, GIVE
ME A POSSESSION OF A BURYING PLACE WITH YOU,
THAT I MAY BURY MY DEAD OUT OF MY SIGHT. OR
THOSE RIGHTEOUS UPON THE TOWER IN SILOAM
FELL AND SLEW THEM, THINK YE THAT THEY WERE
SINNERS ABOVE ALL THE MEN IN JERUSALEM? I
TELL YOU, NAY, BUT EXCEPT YE REPENT, YE SHALL
ALL LIKEWISE PERISH.

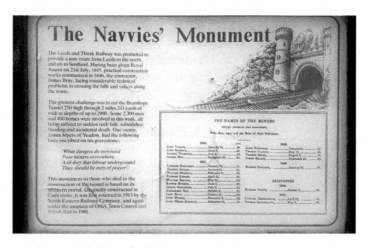

A memorial card later displayed by the Otley Council listing the names, ages and date of demise of those who died, but it is incomplete. Unfortunately the writings of the Rev. Joshua Hart, on which the information is based, has long been lost and nothing else was known – until the finding of the information in this book. (Courtesy of Otley Council and Museum)

There are no names and no numbers written on the monument, but in 1989 Otley Council carried out a refurbishment of the monument and placed a plaque on the railings nearby, identifying some of the men. The names are believed to be taken from the writings of Joshua Hart, vicar of Otley from 1837 to 1865, who conducted the inauguration service.[9]

It is clear, however, that this is not the definitive list for those who died in the tunnel. That list would also include Gaythorpe Firth, a labourer; John Wood, engine attendant; 'a young man of the name of Cawthrs aged 18, a native of Yeadon'; and those who were killed between 1845 and 1846, the years before this record starts. Including James Myers, a miner buried at Yeadon, the total of those now known to have been killed in the tunnel is twenty-seven, although there still may be more to be included in that total of thirty-four stated by Joshua Hart.

Queensbury Tunnel – A Real Monster

Railway accidents of all kinds featured heavily in the local, national and sometimes international newspapers of the times throughout the nineteenth century; sometimes two or three were reported in the same day. Papers recreated the circumstances often in graphic, even what we might call gory, and intimate detail. Sometimes they became almost blasé in their reportage so numerous and repetitive were these accidents, but they were also the means whereby the railway companies were held to task in the public arena. Using their own vernacular and their own local or specialist knowledge, they give us is an insight into the back stories that surrounded these operations – 'he was taken to the dead-house at the Workhouse' or 'but lockjaw set in' (grist to a social historian's mill, putting the accident into its context) – as well as giving us the reality of what it was like to be there working in and on those tunnels. Perhaps the real value of this reportage, however, is that it truly highlights the ultimate human cost of railway progress.

At 430ft (131m) below the village of the same name, on the Bradford, Halifax and Thornton Railway line, Queensbury Tunnel's claim to fame today is that it is the longest and deepest disused tunnel in England.[10] At its opening in 1878, however, according to a contemporary journalist who strolled through the tunnel as navvies made their finishing touches, 'the pyramids of Egypt sink into insignificance compared to it'.[11] That might sound rather extravagant viewed from the twenty-first century, but there can be no doubt that the tunnel – opened in 1878 – still stands as a monument to the determination and courage exhibited by railway engineers during the Victorian era. By any standards, it was a considerable achievement: 'the magnitude of the work, of the engineering skill required, and of the innumerable difficulties to be overcome, in making those almost two miles of railway.'[12]

With such a depth the tunnel created its own surprising problems: huge icicles formed on the ceiling. These often damaged locos passing through. To combat this, engines were sometimes left running in the tunnel to prevent them from forming. The large, cold, dank space held onto the smoke and steam, which formed moist clouds so dense that drivers failed to realise they were nearing the end of the tunnel at Queensbury Station. To alert them to this, a huge gong was installed – the arm of which was struck by the front of the train! Amazingly the remnants of this fitting are still there in the tunnel today.[13]

Work on the tunnel began on 21 May 1874 when four observatories were erected, from which a view was commanded over each of the intended eight construction shafts (although only seven were sunk). Shaft No. 8 – the northernmost shaft – was first to be started. As with many tunnels, water proved a considerable hindrance and the ample pumping provision was almost defeated on several occasions due to heavy rain. Indeed, Nos 5 and 6 shafts had to be abandoned to the water when sunk to depths of 266ft (81m) and 196ft (60m) respectively.[14] The creation of this massive, cavernous monster of a tunnel made enormous demands of the men who worked it. They faced injury, maiming, suffocation and sometimes death, which was, in turn, reported in a matter-of-fact (at times almost casual) way by the local papers:

Bradford Observer, Monday 12 October 1874
FATAL ACCIDENT AT QUEENSBURY

On Saturday evening a fatal accident occurred on the Halifax, Thornton and Keighley Railway, at No.1 Shaft near Beggarington, Queensbury. The shaft is being sunk for driving the tunnel under Queensbury in connection with the above railway, and is worked by a semi-portable engine. The iron cage had been raised to the mouth of the pit, which had also been covered up, when for some unexplained reason the engine-tender, Thomas Dyson, started his engine, and drew the cage up to the pulley, where the rope broke, setting free the cage, which broke through the wooden doors at the top of the shaft and fell to the bottom, striking three men who were down at work. One of them, *Richard Sutcliffe,* a sinker, aged thirty, of Range Bank, Halifax, was struck on the head and instantly killed. Two other men, named *John Price* and *Thomas Dyson*, masons, were also severely injured. They were taken to the Halifax Infirmary, and Dyson is reported to have died since. The inquest will be held tomorrow at the Royal Oak Inn, Ambler Thorn.

Halifax Courier, Saturday 10 July 1875
ANOTHER FATAL ACCIDENT ON THE HALIFAX, THORNTON AND KEIGHLEY RAILWAY

Shortly before nine o'clock yesterday morning, a banksman, named *Sutcliffe Hodgson*, aged twenty-seven, and residing at Priestley Hill, near Queensbury, was killed under shocking circumstances at No.1 shaft on the works of the tunnel near that village for the Bradford, Halifax and Thornton Railway.

The landing stage on which he was standing at the time of the accident had been drawn back from the mouth of the shaft, and the catch not having been put on, it slipped back about eighteen inches, causing him to fall headlong down the shaft, which is forty-four yards deep, into the tunnel. He was killed instantly. About seventeen feet from the bottom some scaffolding was fixed, a plank of which he broke in his fall, and those who went to his assistance had to go round by the adjoining shaft in order to get at the place.

The body was taken up in a fearfully mangled condition, the head having been knocked quite flat, and many bones broken. It was carried to his house at Priestley Hill, where its arrival caused considerable excitement in the neighbourhood, to which his family also belonged. He leaves a young wife, to whom he was married quite recently.

Bradford Observer, Thursday 2 September 1875
ANOTHER ACCIDENT ON THE LINE

Another accident happened at the Halifax, Thornton, and Bradford Railway on Sunday evening. It appears that fitters having fixed an additional pipe 9in long and 12in bore to the pump in connection with No.4 shaft of the Queensbury tunnel, had taken out the spear rods by which the pump is worked, to make the necessary addition to their length.

Two men named *George Waite* and *George Parker* were engaged in lowering them down again into the shaft by the aid of a capstan, when the weight (about four tons) overpowered them, and Waite was whirled violently round three or four times by the handle of the capstan, and then thrown off. When taken up it was found that one leg was broken below the knee, the bone protruding through his dress. In a short time a conveyance was procured, and he was removed to the Halifax Infirmary. Parker after being taken once round was cast onto the metals of the adjoining tramway fortunately not much worse.

Halifax Courier, Saturday 18 March 1876
FATAL ACCIDENT IN THE QUEENSBURY TUNNEL

Yesterday, an inquest was held by Mr Barstow, coroner, at

Armstrong's Hotel, Bradford, respecting the death of *Richard Jones*, who died from injuries received while at work in the Queensbury Tunnel on the Bradford, Halifax and Thornton Railway. The deceased, who was thirty-three years of age, went under another name upon the works – a custom not uncommon upon navvies.

On Monday last he and two other men were at work at the Hole Bottom end of the tunnel, and after firing some shots the deceased returned to the place to clear away a loose piece of rock which was in the way of another drilling. For this purpose, he used a 'pick', and after working at the stone for some little time, his companions called to him to come away or the stone would be upon him. Their warning came too late, however, for as Jones was making his escape the stone, weighing about 4cwt, fell upon him, and crushed him terribly.

Assistance being readily at hand the unfortunate man was extricated, and sent to the Bradford Infirmary, but he died on arriving in the neighbourhood to Lister Hills. After being seen by Dr Lee, whose surgery was close at hand, the deceased's remains were taken to the dead-house at the Workhouse. Several of his fellow-workmen were called, but no blame seemed to attach to anyone, except perhaps the deceased himself, and the verdict arrived at was 'Accidental death'.

Bradford Observer, Saturday 3 June 1876
ACCIDENT IN THE TUNNEL

On Tuesday morning, one of the men employed in the tunnel at Hole Bottom met with an accident while at work. It appears in traversing the scaffold on which the masons work, he unwittingly stepped on the loose end of a plank, which tilted and caused him to fall into the bottom of the tunnel. He sustained severe injuries about the head and back, and one arm was badly crushed. He was conveyed to his home in Wheatley, where he is progressing favourably.

Halifax Courier, Saturday 5 August 1876

FATAL RESULT OF AN ACCIDENT

On Thursday morning, a young man, named *Llewellyn Jones*, died at Queensbury from injuries received on the Halifax, Thornton, and Bradford Railway. Deceased was employed as a miner in the tunnel at No.2 shaft. On the morning of the 17th inst, he commenced drilling a hole which had been left by the men on the night shift in ignorance of its being charged, when it exploded and severely injured him about the right arm and face. He was assisted home and medical aid obtained, and up to Tuesday last appeared to be progressing favourably, when lock-jaw set in, and all the efforts of the medical men proved futile, the deceased expiring on Thursday morning in great agony.

Halifax Courier, Saturday 26 August 1876

RAILWAY ACCIDENT

Last Saturday morning another accident happened in Queensbury Tunnel, by which two men named *Herbert Evans* and *John Newstead* received severe injuries. It appears Evans, who is a bricklayer, was preparing to come down from the top scaffold on which he was working, when he missed his footing and fell to the bottom, a distance of nine yards, sustaining serious injury about the spine. A labourer going up the ladder at the time, with a piece of timber on his shoulder, was so startled by the occurrence that he let the timber fall and hit Newstead, cutting him badly about the head and face. Both men were brought out at No.3 shaft, and conveyed to their lodgings. Medical assistance was immediately sent for and they are both reported to be progressing favourably.

Halifax Guardian, Saturday 9 February 1878

SERIOUS ACCIDENT, YESTERDAY

Another accident of a very serious nature occurred yesterday at the tunnel under Queensbury, to an excavator named *Thomas Williams*. He is a Welshman, and whilst working in the tunnel a piece of rock fell upon him, and severely injured him. He was conveyed to the Halifax Infirmary, and it is feared his back is broken.[15]

When Queensbury Tunnel was completed it was, no doubt, to the relief of not only the contractors and sub-contractors and the Board and stockholders of the company, but also to the hundreds of navvies who had worked there and the sorrow of the families of the men who had died there.

Pity the Poor Platelayer!

Question: (a) who or (b) what was a 'platelayer'?
Answer: (a) a 'platelayer' was a male (women only did this job during the Second World War) railway employee; (b) their job was to maintain 'the permanent way' (in early times this identified it against tracks that were temporary rail lines often laid when work was in progress).

Once a railway was built, the railway company employed platelayers to maintain the line, including all the parts that went into the rail track, such as the sleepers, chairs, ballast and rails. The name derives from the early 'plateways', the predecessors

Platelayers were an essential category of worker on the railways, although looked upon as low down the scale of importance. It was a job that placed the men in imminent danger at almost all times, hence the need for a lookout, although this was not always provided for in the early years. Even when such a man was part of the company's policy, they were often disregarded by the workmen themselves.

of railway tracks. These worked like rail tracks but used iron (or wooden) plates with a vertical flange on the inside or the outside, the wagon wheels having no flange. Sometimes they were given a particular length of track to maintain and they would have a little hut alongside it. Working long hours – twelve hours a day, six days a week – each day the platelayer set out along his section of track, loaded down with a pick, a shovel, hammers, spanners and track-measuring gauges. His sharp eyes picked out any imperfection, from broken or uneven rails, to rails that were too wide or too narrow. It wasn't just the track that had to be kept in order, the platelayer was expected to repair fences and keep ditches clear as well.[16] Often, in later times, they worked in gangs under a 'ganger' – a foreman or chargeman in other industries – and each gang was responsible for the maintenance of a particular length of track.

It was a very necessary and important job ensuring the safe passage of the train over the track, but it was also a lowly labourer's job and little thought was given to the safety of the platelayer. Will Thorne, a Victorian platelayer, in correspondence with author Frank McKenna, stated that the platelayer was 'the most neglected man in the service'. A witness giving evidence in a Crystal Palace Tunnel accident stated:

> When two trains passed through the tunnel simultaneously, as upon this occasion, the men engaged in repairing the metals had to lie down at full length in the six-foot way or between the near rail and the wall [the four-foot way], as there was no other means provided for their safety.

Both places were very perilous positions to be in. In some tunnels there were 'manholes', small arches scraped out of the wall, which were able to fit two or three men into the space.

Reading through newspapers of the period, official reports and railway magazines such as *The Railway Review* – a weekly newspaper of the railway service – there are graphic descriptions of the many fatal accidents involving platelayers.

It would appear that the platelayer, going about his daily work, was in constant peril, especially in tunnels. The abundance of accidents and fatalities bear witness to this. What is also horribly obvious in reading the coroner's court reports is that very little was done to eliminate or diminish these happenings, or to carry out the jury's recommendations for improvements, especially when they return the verdict 'Accidental Death', which means no one was to blame, with monotonous regularity.

Islington Gazette, Tuesday 27 December 1870
TWO DIE IN TUNNEL

A gang of twenty something had been working on 'relaying the rails' in the tunnel for around ten days at Wheatstone Tunnel, between Colney Hatch and Barnet Stations on the Great Northern Railway. At about 9.20 on Wednesday morning, 21 December 1870, they 'were at work placing new chairs, sleepers and rails on the up-line, about 150 yards inside the tunnel. A luggage train going to London entered the tunnel … fog signals were placed at the mouth of the tunnel and one went off before the luggage train entered. The foreman shouted "stand clear" and the whole gang passed from the up-line over the six foot and stood against the wall of the down-line until the train had past. It filled the tunnel with smoke.' Directly after this train had passed, in less than a minute, a train due at Barnet dashed pass at about 30 miles per hour. When it was gone it was seen that 'someone was knocked down'. Lights were brought and, going towards the Barnet end of the tunnel, they saw *John Britnall,* aged 32 years, 'with his feet near the metals and his head against the wall. He was quite dead.' A few yards further the body of *Joseph Dearman*, aged 27 years, was found in the same position. Sydney Britnall, the deceased's brother, who was working a little way off from him, said he 'happened to turn his head before the down train had passed, or he would have been killed too. It was a wonder that the whole of the men had not gone from the wall onto the down-line when the luggage train passed' as they would all have been killed. The men had chosen to stand against the wall because they 'could not lie in the six foot [usual practice] because the ballast and sleepers were lying there'.

Mr Richard Johnson, the engineer to the Company, told the Inquest that: 'from the wall to the metals it was 3 feet 2 inches. The wall was on the incline and 14 inches was left for the men to stand between the wall and the metal.'

Mr Berry, MRCS, told the Inquest that he had examined Dearman and found: 'the top of the skull was completely cut, particularly on the right side. The brain had entirely escaped and the bones of the face were all broken, as was his left thigh.' On examining Britnall he found exactly the same injuries but from the left side.' He believed Dearman had been struck first and he in turn had struck Britnall who was turned around.

George Soulton, driver of the 9.25 down-train told the Court he had 'blown his whistle before entering the tunnel' … he knew nothing of the accident but on returning to Kings Cross and examining the engine 'he found a piece of flesh on it.'

Both of the deceased had worked for the company for some years and were much respected; both were married men with families and the court was informed that 'the company would provide for them.'

The Railway Review, 1881

KNOCKED DOWN LIKE SO MANY NINEPINS …
These are the words of Coroner, Mr William Carter, who led the lengthy inquiry (at two separate inquests because they died at different times) into the fatal accident that took place in the Crystal Palace Tunnel of the London, Brighton, and South Coast Railway Company, on Thursday .

Platelayer *Jonathan Bissex*, aged 32 years (died at the scene), and platelayer *Joseph Fuller* (died later in St George's Hospital) were part of a 3-man gang working in the tunnel.

Charles Sharman, the last member of the gang, was the principal witness at the Inquest. He told the Court:

They entered at Gipsy-hill end, and commenced work on the down line from Victoria to the Crystal Palace. They had naphtha lamps, which they shifted about as they wanted. After breakfast they again entered the tunnel for the purpose of lifting some 'joints' on the load. About two hours after they had resumed work witness noticed a goods train enter the tunnel from the Crystal Palace end. As witness was standing against the wall looking at the goods train they all became enveloped in steam and smoke, and as it passed witness felt a man thrown against his legs. That was the first intimation he had of a second train being in the tunnel.

Witness soon after found that it was a London and North-Western passenger train from Willesden Junction to New and South Croydon, due at the Crystal Palace Station at 10.35 p.m.

Witness could not say at what rate it was going. He could not hear its approach on account of the noise from the goods train. After the train had passed they were left in total darkness, the lamps having been extinguished by the engine of the passenger train.

Witness was of opinion that the drive of the passenger train could not see them. He did not hear any whistle sounded by the passenger train. It was usual for drivers to sound the whistle at either end of the tunnel. He believed the goods train was a very heavy one on account of having two engines. If the whistle had been sounded witness was of opinion that he should not have heard it owing to the noise caused by the puffs of the engine and the rattling of the trucks. [The driver of the passenger train proved he 'whistled' three times before entering the tunnel.]

As soon as the trains passed witness he stooped down and felt a man at his feet. He took hold of him and said, 'Who are you?' He received no answer, and soon after

he came across the other man, and he received no reply
from him.

Witness then had to grope his way out of the tunnel in the
dark, when he saw Walter Mitchell with a light in his hand.
They then went to the signal-box, and gave information to
the signalman. He then went back with Mitchell, when they
found the deceased. They removed him on one side. A few
yards further on they discovered Fuller alive, but unconscious.

When two trains passed through the tunnel simultaneously,
as upon this occasion, the men engaged in repairing the
metals had to lie down at full length in 'the six-foot way' or
between the near rail and the wall ' the four-foot' way as there
was no other means provided for their safety. Sharman told
the Court that in his opinion the accident was unpreventable
so far as the driver of the passenger train was concerned. Had
there been any recesses in the tunnel he could not say, under
the circumstances, whether he or the deceased men would
have got into them. There were no air shafts in the tunnel.
There had been when he first worked in the tunnel but they
had since been filled in.

The jury's verdict: 'Accidental death', adding the following
rider:

> That the tunnel in question was highly dangerous to
> the men working in it, and to prevent further loss of life
> they [the jury] would suggest that, an air shaft should be
> provided; also that man-holes should be made so as to
> enable the men to get out in safety instead of lying down
> on the ballast, thereby exposing themselves to be scalded to
> death; and also, while the line was under repair, the drivers
> should be instructed to slacken speed while passing through
> the tunnel.

They returned the same 'Accidental death' verdict for Joseph
Fuller, adding:

'Manholes', as they were called – a scoop out of the wall able to hold, in theory, two to three men, sometimes lined, sometimes not, spaced out down the tunnel – were the supposed places of refuge. Sometimes they were just not deep enough or far enough away from the track, or the men were unable to reach them in time; but, they were better than nothing. Even so it must have been somewhat alarming standing with your back to the wall in the darkness and feel an express train speed pass you literally feet away. (Courtesy of Phill Davison)

That on every occasion of a train passing through a tunnel
when men were working in it, the same precautions should
be taken as if the line was broken up, and a man should be
stationed outside the tunnel with a suitable lamp and flag,
thus denoting the fact of men being employed at the time
in the tunnel. [17]

Sapperton Tunnel

HC Deb 27 April 1896, Vol. 39 c. 1732–33
MR CHANNING
PLATELAYERS IN DANGEROUS POSITIONS
I beg to ask the President of the Board of Trade, whether
the Board of Trade was represented at the inquest held
at Stroud, on 16 April, on the four platelayers killed in
Sapperton Tunnel on 14 April, or have ordered an inspector
or sub-inspector to inquire into the circumstances; and, if
not, whether he will cause such inquiry to be held with
a view to authoritative recommendations by the Board of
Trade as to the precautions necessary for the safety of platelayers in dangerous positions?

A gang of twenty-six platelayers and packers out of Swindon
were working in Sapperton Tunnel, which lies four miles east
of Stroud, on the evening of Tuesday 4 April 1896. They were
working on levelling the ballast on the down-line. Charles
Warren, a packer, second man in the gang, and a main witness
at the Inquest, told how he had been sent by the ganger,
Frederick Gee, to the Swindon end of the long tunnel as 'lookout' and to shout out the Down train. At the approach of the
down-express, some half a mile off, he went back down into
the tunnel to shout the warning 'Down train'. The tunnel was
full of steam and smoke as an up-goods had just gone through.
He said he heard the men answer and believed everything was
fine. After the down express entered the tunnel he stepped

Presumably a lookout man for a gang working inside Sapperton Tunnel. Board of Trade railway inspectors were always demanding that this should be the case in order to prevent accidents. The problem for the platelayers, however, was that the lookout was ineffective, as there was not one at each end. (Courtesy of Howard Beard, Chair of the Stroud Local History Society)

back outside, he told the court, but in just a few minutes a man named Ford appeared and said something had happened. Warren got a light and they went back into the tunnel. Things must have happened very quickly, and suddenly, as the men had managed to get safely out of the way of a down train, but were 'run down by an up-ballast train'. Two of the men, H. J. Ballard (36) and E. Greenway (25), died immediately from their horrendous injuries. Greenway had to be 'pulled out from under the material train, having been pushed a

distance of 50 yards'.[18] The dead men were put in the guards
van attached to the engine of the 'material train' and taken
back to Brimscombe. Three others were injured – the ganger,
F. Gee (48), 'had his left arm cut off and his skull very severely
fractured'; although alive when found, he did not speak, and
died on the way from Stroud to the hospital, leaving a widow
and nine children. W. Poynter was bleeding from the nose, but
able to return to his home later that evening; however, he died
of his injuries just a few days later. The fifth man, J Hillsley,
sustained concussion of the brain, scalp wounds and bruised
limbs. He told the Inquest that they had been working using
naptha lamps fixed on stands. He had moved out of the way
of the down train and had made for the wall on the up road,
carrying his lamp. It was hard to see because the tunnel was
full of smoke. Before he got to the wall, the ballast train came
up and the engine caught his elbow and knocked him against
the wall. He neither saw nor heard anything to warn him of
the approach of this train. 'They had known it was coming
as they were used to the material train coming to take them
home at night, but had not expected it so soon.'

The injured were transported to Stroud on a passenger
train which passed through shortly after. Some of the gang
that were standing elsewhere were unharmed but all were
stunned 'at the shocking end of their fellows'.[19] It caused great
agitation in Stroud and large numbers came onto the streets
outside the hospital.

The jury's verdict: accidental death. They added the rider,
recommending:

> when platelayers are working in tunnels a look-out man
> should be stationed on both lines. No look out had been
> posted on the up trains with the result that the ballast train
> ran into the gang before its approach was noticed because
> of the noise and smoke which attended the passage of the
> down train through the tunnel.[20]

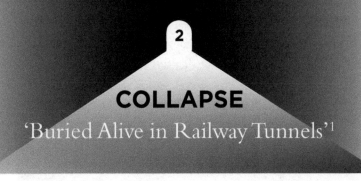

COLLAPSE
'Buried Alive in Railway Tunnels'[1]

'Tunnel collapsed', 'buried alive' – these phrases bring the heart into the throat of those whose loved ones were in those tunnels. One of the most vulnerable parts of a tunnel, liable to collapse, are the shafts. A shaft, in appearance, was very much like an ordinary well. It was a wide, deep, vertical hole dug down into the ground at some point along the tunnel's trajectory.

At the bottom they are usually lined in timber. From the base of each shaft the tunnel was excavated and supported until a side length of around 15ft (4.5m) was formed in each direction. This was built with a lining much thicker than the rest of the tunnel as it had to support the weight of the shaft as well as itself. This practice left the tunnel vulnerable as, until the lining was completed, the weight of the shaft was supported only on the timbers.

The required number of shafts was sunk at regular and reasonable distances apart along the alignment of the proposed tunnel. The shafts served several purposes:

1) access to and out of the tunnel, especially useful in an emergency;
2) the means to convey men and equipment up and down to the tunnel floor;
3) as ventilation openings both during and after the tunnel construction;

This lithograph by well-known railway artist J.C. Bourne was shown on the cover of *Literary World: A Journal of Popular Information and Entertainment* (No. 12, Saturday 22 June 1839) accompanying an article on the London & Birmingham Railway – the longest and greatest line at that time. It had eight tunnels along its length; the longest, most impressive and notorious was Kilsby at 2,443 yards long.

So long was Kilsby Tunnel that it excited the anxieties of the public and scientific men, who believed that passengers could well be suffocated 'from smoke and lack of air'. To overcome this apprehension (and perhaps any chance of it actually happening) ventilation shafts were built (as was the practice on other tunnels too). Kilsby Tunnel is known not least because of this vast shaft 60ft in diameter and 132ft deep; its walls are perpendicular, and 3ft thick throughout. Nowadays people like to stand on the grid on top of the shaft and get the 'Kilsby blow' experience from the train passing below.

4) sometimes with particularly long tunnels 'sighting shafts' were also dug.

Steining was a method by which shafts were sunk like wells and walled as the hole was being dug (such as at Sapperton Tunnel):

> The bottom-most circle of masonry was built first, on top of a wooden curb, on top of the hill. As the earth was excavated beneath it the whole growing cylinder of masonry sank into the growing hole. The stone lining in fact was lowered ring by ring into the earth. The first-laid circle of masonry ended at the shaft bottom.[2]

What is a Heading?

A heading is the name given to the beginnings of a tunnel or heading that headed out from the shaft. Sometimes there could be a top and bottom heading.

Watford Tunnel – Buried Alive

The making of the London and Birmingham Railway was one of the great engineering feats of the time and it aroused a lot of interest amongst the engineering fraternity and drew much admiration, such as that of Lieutenant Peter Lecount RN, a member of Stephenson's project team who wrote:

> The London and Birmingham Railway is unquestionably the greatest public work ever executed, either in ancient or modern times. If we estimate its importance by the labour alone which has been expended on it, perhaps the Great Chinese Wall might compete with it; but when we consider the immense outlay of capital which it has required – the great and varied talents which have been in a constant state

of requisition during the whole of its progress – together with the unprecedented engineering difficulties, which we are happy to say are now overcome – the gigantic work of the Chinese sinks totally into the shade.[3]

There are several written insights into the problems encountered:

The gravel is most abundant in the neighbourhood of Watford, covering the upper chalk which in many places it penetrates, or in other words, the large fissures or rents in the chalk are filled with gravel, and as this latter material is very loose and mobile, it was the occasion of much difficulty and danger in the excavation of the Watford tunnel; for at times, when the miners thought they were excavating through solid chalk, they would in a moment break into loose gravel, which would run into the tunnel with the rapidity of water, unless the most prompt precautions were taken.[4]

We also have some technical facts:

… the entrance to the Watford Tunnel; it is 24 feet wide, and the crown of the arch is 25 feet high; it is ventilated by six shafts, *the largest of which is a memorial of the death of the persons buried here during the excavation;*[5] the shaft was increased in size to get out their bodies; the tunnel is one mile 170 yards in length; upwards 120,000 cubic yards of earth were taken out of it.[6]

We are fortunate to have a glimpse inside Watford Tunnel at the time of its construction, written by H.J. Brown, a highly articulate navvy who worked there as a young lad aged 16:

… There was no day there and no peace: the shrill roar of escaping steam; the groans of mighty engines heaving ponderous loads of earth to the surface; the click-clack of lesser engines pumping dry the numerous springs by which the drift was intersected; the reverberating thunder of the small blasts of powder fired upon the mining works; the rumble of trains of trucks; the clatter of horses' feet; the clank of chains; the strain of cordage; and a myriad of other sounds, accordant and discordant. There were to be seen miners from Cornwall, drift-borers from Wales, pitmen from Staffordshire and Northumberland, engineers from Yorkshire and Lancashire, navvies – Englishmen, Scotchmen, and Irishmen – from everywhere, muck-shifters, pickmen, barrowmen, brakes-men, banksmen, drivers, gaffers, gangers, carpenters, bricklayers, labourers, and boys of all sorts, ages and sizes; some engaged upon the inverts beneath the rails, some upon the drains below these, some upon the extension of the drifts, some clearing away the falling earth, some loading it upon the trucks, some working like bees in cells building up the tunnel sides, some upon the centre turning the great arches, some stretched upon their backs putting the key-bricks to the crown – all speaking in a hundred dialects, with dangers known and unknown impending on every side; with commands and countermands echoing about through air murky with the smoke and flame of burning tar-barrels, cressets, and torches. Such was the interior of Watford tunnel.[7]

Watford Tunnel highlights the problem of working a tunnel out into headings from the sunk shaft. The side lengths were being built when a collapse occurred. This resulted in not only the section of tunnel being lost, but also the shaft being brought down, as it was then only supported by the timbers, the important part of the lining having not been completed yet.[8] On 17 July 1835 the shocking accident occurred. Several men – the number is written up variously as nine, ten, eleven or fourteen – lost their lives. What is not known is whether they were killed outright. What people wonder is: might some have survived the collapse only to die due to asphyxiation? Working in the tunnel was H.J. Brown, who experienced the reality of the disaster. Brown was fortunate in his career as a navvy, as he lived to tell the tale, and he had many disasters to write about:

> Later in the summer occurred that terrible disaster by which upwards of thirty men, were buried alive by the in-falling of a mass of earth. Fourteen were not rescued until life was extinct, and the last body not recovered until after a lapse of three weeks. Of those who were rescued alive, all, with the exception of one man, sustained more or less of corporeal injury – fractures, contusions, and bruises. This man, who owed his rescue to having been at work beneath some shelving planks when the earth fell in, was taken out crazed, and died shortly after a raving madman.
>
> The scene was terrible. Above yawned an abyss, down which huge trees had been carried, for it was woodland here above the tunnel; the trunks of many had been snapped like sticks, and the roots of some were branching up into the air. Below, on either side of the mass, were gangs of brave, daring men – the navvie is a bold fellow when danger is to be faced – endeavouring to work their way through it. Day and night, for one-and-twenty days, these labours unremittingly continued, until at length the body of the last victim was found.[9]

Not surprisingly the accident was covered extensively by several local papers anxious to give the fullest details. Their writings are graphic recordings of the horrendous story:

> The shaft in question, one of the four in this length of tunnel (1,700 yards), is termed a gin-shaft, and has been sunk about 90 feet below an elevated platform erected for the purpose of removing the earth. The shaft has been very lately sunk, and two nine-feet lengths of tunnel had been bricked, the third being, it is stated, just mined and ready for the bricklayers. The shaft was about to be bricked on Friday morning, between 5 and 6 o'clock, by a party consisting of five bricklayers and six

labourers, who composed what is termed the night gang; and had the appalling event taken place a few hours afterwards, the morning gang would have been at work, and the loss of human life must have been awful in the extreme ... In loosening a portion of the wood work previous to bricking the shaft, it is supposed the earth gave way and buried the unfortunate men, carrying the whole of the wood work with it ... The men must be buried upwards of 80 feet below the surface of the earth, and although 60 men are actively engaged in digging out the bodies, it is probable that six or seven days will elapse before they are extricated.[10]

When the tunnel collapsed a horse and gin were partly buried beneath the earth. When the horse was finally extracted, it was discovered that the poor animal had sustained serious injury. Fortunately 'the man attending to the gin heard some of the earth in the shaft fall, and, feeling the ground under his feet giving way, he made a precipitate retreat, and providentially escaped, while a dog that was lying by his side did not and was buried with the earth'.[11]

Unfortunately no one could attempt any form of rapid rescue as there was now no shaft down which they could gain access; one had to be constructed:

After more than a month of incessant exertions on the part of Messrs. Harding and Copeland, the contractors for the Watford line of the London and Birmingham Railway, and a vast number of labourers who were relieved every twelve hours, the bodies of some of the unfortunate men, who were buried under more than eighty feet of earth, by the sudden falling in of the shaft in Russell Wood, Levesdon Green, Watford, in this county, have been dug out. Early on Saturday morning the miners were enabled by crawling between the interstices made by the fallen timbers, to see the legs of some of the sufferers, and to know that before many more feet of the gravel and chalk had been removed (the distance from the surface being about eighty-four feet) they would come to the bodies … At three o'clock in the afternoon an extended hand presented itself to the view of the bystanders, on the side of the opening opposite to that which the first eruption of the gravel is supposed to have taken place. The body on being cleared was found in a sitting posture, with the head thrown back; it is presumed the poor fellow was looking upwards at the moment he met his death, have heard the cry of 'ware' from the men at the top of the arch; his face was crushed and the legs broken.[12]

On Monday 11 August 'the dog belonging to the man attending to the "gin" was dug out', and on Wednesday 'a basket containing some bread' was retrieved. Eventually they reached the men.

The first body taken out was lying on one of the bars – a piece of timber about 15cm (6in) in diameter. He was in a horizontal position, with the whole weight of the gravel upon him; his hands were extended and his knees bent up. The third body was found in the immediate vicinity of the others; it was discovered that his bowels had burst by the sudden pressure of the timber upon him. The fourth sufferer was lying amongst the centres, crushed by the gravel. The fifth body was found with the head fixed fast in one of the centres in a downward position. The sixth was lying with his back upwards and his left hand bent under him.[13]

Coroner's Inquest on Nine Men Killed at the Watford Tunnel

On Monday 17 August, the 'most respectable jury' met at the pub, the Essex Arms, Watford, to carry out the coroner's inquest. Those that met to 'inquire into the cause of death of nine men killed by the falling in of the part of the tunnel-forming in Russell Wood', near Watford, comprised:

Thomas Jordan – overlooker, widower
Joseph [James] Barker – foreman, miner

Thomas Evans – bricklayer, unmarried
Silvanes Rudlings/Reubens – bricklayer, unmarried
John Betts/Clarke – bricklayer, unmarried
William Byrd – bricklayer, unmarried
Thomas Winmill – labourer, married
James Darvell – labourer
Bartlett Jeans

The jury proceeded to view the bodies of the men that had been transferred to the engine house, in the hope of preventing contamination from the decomposed bodies. 'They presented a most sad spectacle,' one member reported. After a detailed discussion, which is recorded as 'add[ing] nothing to the information already known to the public', the jury brought forth a verdict of accidental death. Maybe the court had not heard enough evidence. They should have called the young lad H.J. Brown, for he had a definite opinion:

> The causes assigned for the accident were conflicting; and, as is usual in such cases, each party did their best to fix the blame upon the other – the engineers upon the contractors, these upon their sub-contractors, and these again upon those beneath them.
>
> I believe that the disaster was really attributable to a foreman of bricklayers, who madly, and against orders, drew away the centering of some newly-turned arches; the earth followed; and the doomed men beneath – presuming the cause I have given to be the right one – became the victims of a drunken man's temerity.

The jury also stated they believed 'that every possible care and attention that skill and science could dictate, had been used on the part of the Company, their agents and superintendents, in the construction of the shafts and works that had been brought to their notice'. The bodies of the unfortunate victims were buried that day in Watford churchyard.[14]

Such was the now known risk of tunnelling through this hazardous terrain that the men were, not unsurprisingly, reluctant to continue. Writing in 1904, Francis Fox, the son of the tunnel's resident engineer, Charles Fox, recalled his father's strategy for getting the men back to work:

> Whilst engaged in the construction of the Watford Tunnel, he received instructions to go to Birmingham. He asked to be allowed to remain, for they were working in very soft and dangerous ground; but his request was declined, and he was sent to Birmingham. He had not been gone more than a few days when a message was received that the tunnel had fallen in, and eleven men had been killed. He immediately hurried back, and found that there was a panic on the spot. Up to this point is what my father himself told me, but a very old friend of mine further related that, when the tunnel had fallen in and had produced this panic, my father went to the works and said to the men, 'That tunnel has to be put through, cost what it will, and therefore I want you men to volunteer.' Not one of them would do so. 'Very well,' he said, 'I will do it'; and he got into the bucket, and was just about to be lowered down the shaft, when the ganger, using language more strong than elegant, said he 'would not see the master killed alone.' He went down with him, and these two finished the length through the dangerous ground, after which the men returned to work.[15]

By February 1837, the chairman was able to report that all that now needed to be done on the Watford Tunnel was a small amount of work on the excavations at either end.

Northchurch Tunnel – 'First Lives Lost'

Tunnelling was the civil engineer's nightmare, for it was impossible to foresee with confidence what lay beneath the

VIEW OF NORTH CHURCH TUNNEL, LONDON & BIRMINGHAM RAILWAY.
Shewing the works in state of progress as they appeared in September 1837.

A beautiful depiction of North Church Tunnel, as it is written here. The air of country tranquillity and calmness belies the activity and energy that would have been going on. (Courtesy of Chris Heavens)

surface. Subterranean streams and, worse still, pockets of quicksand and gravel might be concealed, which, when pierced, would pour into the workings in a torrent until the cavity it occupied was empty. Then, no longer able to support the weight of the ground above, the cavity would collapse, burying the workings and those unfortunate enough not to have got out in time. This incident occurred during construction on the Northchurch Tunnel, to the south of Tring station:

The soil through which we were carrying the drift of Northchurch tunnel was of a most treacherous character,

Supporting the tunnel inside Northchurch Tunnel was
of vital importance as it was beset with loose quicksand
that could flow like water and then cause a collapse.
(Courtesy of www.gerald-massey.org.uk/railway)

and caused many disasters. Despite every precaution, the
earth would at times fall in, and that, too, when and where
we least expected. Thus, in the fifth week of our contract,
notwithstanding that our shoring was of extra strength
and well strutted, an immense mass of earth suddenly came
down upon us. This came from the tapping of a quicksand.
One stroke of a pick did it. The vein was shelving and the
sand, finding a vent, ran like so much water into the open
drift; which was of course speedily choked up. George
Hatley was at once on the spot; and, under his directions
efforts were promptly made to clear away the sand, so that
the shoring should be re-strengthened if possible before
the earth above (deprived of the support afforded by the
sand) should collapse. The most strenuous efforts were
made in vain. There came a low rumbling, like the distant
booming of artillery, then followed crashes louder than
the thunder, startling us from our labour; and, while we
were hurrying away, down came the whole mass of earth,
masonry, timber, and sand, crushing five men under it. Of
these men three were dug out alive, and removed terribly

mangled – to the West Herts Infirmary; the other two
were found dead.[16]

Once again from the pen of H.J. Brown, who had moved to
the Northchurch Tunnel after leaving Watford, we get a first-
hand view of the experience:

> The soil through which we were carrying the drift of
> Northchurch tunnel was of a most treacherous character,
> and caused many disasters. Despite every precaution, the
> earth would at times fall in, and that, too, when and where
> we least expected. Thus, in the fifth week of our contract,
> notwithstanding that our shoring was of extra strength and well
> strutted, an immense mass of earth suddenly came down upon
> us. This came from the tapping of a quicksand. One stroke of a
> pick did it. The vein was shelving and the sand, finding a vent,
> ran like so much water into the open drift; which was of course
> speedily choked up. George Hatley was at once on the spot;
> and, under his directions efforts were promptly made to clear
> away the sand, so that the shoring should be re-strengthened
> if possible before the earth above (deprived of the support
> afforded by the sand) should collapse. The most strenuous
> efforts were made in vain. There came a low rumbling, like the
> distant booming of artillery, then followed crashes louder than
> the thunder, startling us from our labour; and, while we were
> hurrying away, down came the whole mass of earth, masonry,
> timber, and sand, crushing five men under it.
>
> Of these men three were dug out alive, and removed to
> the West Herts Infirmary; the other two were found dead.
> They belonged to a gang, of which one Hicks or Bungerbo
> was ganger. I have described Frazer as a man terribly profane,
> but Hicks was in this matter his master. These were the first
> lives lost in Northchurch tunnel, and Hicks was overjoyed
> to think that they belonged to his own gang. He looked
> forward to the funeral; and, having organised a subscription
> of a shilling per head throughout all the gangs in the tunnel

Pity the poor Irish reapers who would have, obviously, been sat in the open-topped, low-sided, maybe standing room-only third class. They would have had a wild ride with no chance of remaining inside the wagon on collision.

– which subscription realised twenty pounds – five pounds were set apart to pay for burial of the dead, and the rest was reserved to be spent in rioting and drunkenness.

Wallers Ash Tunnel – 'An Accident of a Frightful Description'

The part of the railway line that passed before, after and through Wallers Ash Tunnel (sometimes called Lickfield Tunnel) already had a deadly reputation. On Monday 4 April 1842 the papers broadcast yet another deadly affair: 'It is our painful duty to announce another calamity on this line of road, attended with loss of life.'[17]

For some time prior to the accident, around six to eight weeks, it had been noted that there was a 'dripping of a chalky appearance' from the roof of the tunnel particularly 30ft from the south or Winchester end. It had also been observed that the earth above the tunnel 'appeared to be giving way' – 'It was then ascertained that previous to the formation of the tunnel, a boring had been made, in this precise spot, to ascertain the depth of soil and this caused a fissure, which being filled in, was, of course, by no means so firm as that around it, and to this was attributed the sinking at the top, and the falling at the bottom.'[18] On the Monday a watchman was placed at the tunnel to keep an eye on what was going on. On Tuesday an inspection was carried out by the principal engineer, accompanied by other senior personnel. A plan to ease the pressure on the affected part was made. Ten men were set to work at the spot above the tunnel, to remove the chalk from the surface up to the extent of the falling in. By 7.50 a.m. that Saturday the men had excavated some 50ft. Then they heard a slight rumbling noise, and the next instant the platform gave way beneath them, and, as described by one of the workers, Gamble, 'they were being sunk in a whirlpool and the earth above closed in on them'.[19] A number of the men had been working inside the tunnel strengthening the arch, but when they heard the rumble they ran for their lives and were unhurt.

Coroner's Court: 'The Question was Whether More Might Not Have Been Done?'

The defendants –

The company	South Western Railway Company.
The tunnel	Waller's-ash-tunnel on the South Western Railway line mid-way between Winchester and Andover road stations, nearly a mile and a half from the village of Mitchell Devon.
Mr Martin	South Western Railway's superintendent.
Mr John Douglas	inspector of the South Western Railway between Winchester and Basingstoke. First received notice of some defect on the Monday morning prior to accident. Reported it to Mr Ogleby.

Mr Joseph Locke   principal engineer of the South Western Railway Company. Having received the information he took a train down on the Tuesday morning and had carried out an examination, climbing up a ladder to make a close inspection, then subsequently devised the plan of action.

Mr John Brassy   sole contractor for managing the line of the SW Rly Company and contractor for constructing that portion of the line in which Waller's-ash-tunnel lies. Also contracted 'on a bond' to repair arches, bridges and tunnels. Had examined the tunnel Wednesday, Thursday and Friday. 'The only apparent defect, down to that time [6 p.m. Friday] was a 'snipping' of the bricks to the depth of about half a brick in the worse places.

Mr Ogleby   Mr Brassy's superintendent. Mr Ogleby was given instructions 'to work the men at the shaft, night and day'.

Mr Thomas Jones   Mr Brassy's principal miner – had been employed in the construction and management of railway for about twelve years, the last almost two years with Mr Brassy. He had never been in this tunnel until the Wednesday prior to the accident but then 'did not consider there was any present danger … Arrived at the tunnel at around 6am Saturday and noted "it was damaged to about four inches and a half" from bricks fallen out. Nothing else happened until about 2/3 minutes before the accident, when some 9 inches in thickness fell. I saw danger and halloed out to the men around me, and we had scarcely got out when the rest of the brickwork ad chalk fell through.'[20]

Board of Trade Accident Report
by Major General C.W. Pasley
Primary Causes: Inadequate workmanship, inadequate tunnel support

Giving evidence to the CC regarding the construction of the tunnel, Joseph Locke described that part where the accident happened as 'a peculiarity in construction':

During the construction of the tunnel, after the excavation and whilst the brickwork was being completed, a large conical-shaped piece of chalk fell from the top of the shaft and formed a kind of dome or cavity of 20 feet over the tunnel. The piece of chalk was not of a perfectly conical shape, but had an irregular side, and was scarcely so wide as the tunnel itself and had a long side. This part of the brickwork, in consequence of the slip, was strengthened, and from that time no change took place 'til Monday. There is no such cavity in any other part of the railway, and the rest of the brickwork fits closely into the chalk or soil.

It is my duty to approve the works before they are made use of and I approved Waller's-ash-tunnel before the line was opened.

Board of Trade Accident Report Summary
The Accident
The first symptoms of danger were observed on Monday, the 28th ultimo, and Mr Locke himself was there early next morning, and gave directions that all the loose chalk, which was evidently pressing upon and deranging the brickwork at the crown of the arch of the tunnel, should be removed from

the top by means of the abovementioned shaft. So long as the arch held together, this was the most judicious measure that could be adopted; but early on Saturday morning last, whilst this work was in progress, several of the bricks composing the lower ring of the arch fell down, followed by those of the rings immediately above; and as the whole appeared on the point of giving way, the foreman of the party of labourers then at work withdrew his men out of the shaft, and mentioned his apprehensions to the foreman of the next gang who came to relieve him. The latter [Ferris], who is represented as a man of excellent character, was unfortunately of a different opinion, and sent his men to work in the shaft as usual, he showing by example of going down into it himself, but in a short time afterwards the whole of the brickwork gave way, followed of course by all the loose chalk from the cavity above it, which falling down with the men who were employed there at the time, caused the death of four of them, while several others were injured.

Board of Trade Accident Report

Secondary Causes: Site staff error

Foreman Price   considered the tunnel 'too dangerous and started to send his men back'. The fall of the brickwork increased between 2 and 4 p.m. Price commun-icated his apprehension to Ferris taking him into the tunnel and showing him two barrows of bricks that had already fallen. Foreman Ferris did not agree and told his men to continue the work from above. (Evidence given to coroner's court.)

The men[21]

James Watmore   married, aged 58 (two sons with him), dug out after four hours' labour, 'was a melancholy sight', died

Charles Nyse   single, aged 20, first to be discovered and 'frightfully crushed', died

James Albert/Allet* single, aged 19/23, was the first found of those buried, when 'excavated' 'found in a standing position with every bone in his body smashed to pieces', died

James Batchelor   single, aged 19–22, thrown to the greatest depth, almost to railroad, last to be dug out – 'quite dead'

Thomas Batchelor   single, aged 24–25, partially buried, had to be taken to Winchester hospital with severe bruising, considered in a dangerous state, severely injured

Charles Knight   married, aged 24, badly injured

Daniel Law/Lawes* single, aged 21, severely injured

John Gamble   single, aged 22, clung to a rope until unable to hold on any longer and then fell about 40ft, had 'severe hurt to the spine', right cheek, arms and hands severely lacerated by the rough stone and chalk as he fell and landed, was carried to his father's home in Mitchel, Devon where he stayed

William Knight: recently married, aged 24, severe bruises to back, head and other parts but not considered in a dangerous condition, was working on same plank as James Batchelor but he 'jumped into a hole in the chalk which gave him some shelter and preserved his life' but still fell a

* variations in different reports

considerable depth and was much injured, he was taken to his residence in Mitchell Devon and attended by Dr Watson and was 'going on well'[22]

John Watmore   aged around 28
(son of James)

Thomas Watmore   aged 19, slightly bruised
(brother of John)

The remains of the dead were conveyed to a small hut over the tunnel and stayed there until the coroner's inquest.

Coroner's Court

Jury's verdict   members of the public – found that the foreman, Henry Ferris, was not 'a fit and competent person to be entrusted with the lives of men in so important a work'.

Mr Todd   the coroner, informed the jury – 'the blame, if any, did not so much attach to Ferris, but the company were in fault in not having left some more intelligent and better educated person to superintend the work. [I] really think persons of that uneducated class should not have been left in charge of so dangerous position.'[23]

The Jury's verdict: 'Accidental Death' in each case with a deodand of 50*s* on the materials that fell. Four dead were identified in official Board of Trade Report, but one died after the report was completed:

Salisbury and Winchester Journal, **Monday 11 April 1842**
LOCAL INTELLIGENCE
One of the labourers who was taken out alive from the Wallers-ash Tunnel on Saturday last, died yesterday in Winchester Hospital.

This was probably Thomas Batchelor, who had been considered to be 'in a dangerous state', bringing the total number of deaths to five.

1854
Bramhope Tunnel – Train Buried

Troubled from its beginning, 1854 brought new misfortune to this fateful tunnel. Just a few years after it opened, a roof collapsed and lives were put at risk. A heavily laden government train, which included an open third-class carriage full of 'Irish reapers', ran into the rubble from the roof-fall: 'they had a lucky escape from being buried alive', and then some were given the scariest ride of their lives!

Buried Alive in Railway Tunnels – Communicated by an Engineer
A railway tunnel on the Leeds Northern Railway has fallen in, impeding a train and then partially burying it. The consequent injuries were not by suffocation in the tunnel, but by collision outside the tunnel as one of the consequences. Why the tunnel – not yet 5 years old – fell in, we have yet to learn; but we can picture to ourselves the horror of a buried train and the sufferers dying in agonies. We believe this is the first instance of the kind after the opening of a line, Death thus, in the process of construction, is the more legitimate thing, for which navvies are paid like coal-miners; and as long as they will take risks not altogether

unavoidable, and their paymasters are content, the public do not interfere. But when risks occur which the public are not paid for and are not capable of estimating, the question becomes very serious. We know that bridges fall down from long-continued vibration, and there is no apparent reason why tunnels similarly constructed should be exempt from the same conditions … The processes of destruction may be several – crushing of the arch from unequal bearing of the super-incumbent weight; percolation of water damaging the brick or stone, and washing out the cement or mortar; undermining the invert, and so on. In addition to these, there is the constant process of vibration by means of the locomotives and trains which may gradually disturb the foundations. This is simply a question of the proportion between moving matter and matter at rest. We all know that London houses bear the vibration of carriages for long periods of years; but the heaviest vibration is that of a coal-waggon of five or six tons, at two and a half miles per hour. A locomotive and tender of some sixty tons, at fifty miles per hour, is a widely different thing. The tunnel that has fallen in is a dry tunnel, manifestly for some reason inadequate; and how are we assured that others are not so likewise? How do we know that all tunnels are not in a gradual process of disintegration, and requiring to be renewed from time to time? Another such accident or two of this most fearful of all accidents, and the public will begin seriously to consider whether it is not better worth their while to construct lines on the surface without tunnels, solely for the use of passengers, with high speed and frequent trains of specific weight, and ample-powered engines of moderate weight, on a system that shall render 'accidents' an almost impossibility; leaving the tunnel lines for slow-running goods … The entombing, the burying alive, some hundred passengers away from the light of heaven, would be a horror not yet generally imagined. We are not alarmists, but we know that accidents arise in crops from the periodical wear of material; and this is one of the possible evils which should be foreseen and prevented after this, our first warning. If another such accident occurs, it will be the fault of the Government Inspectors, for want of due examination. It is usually the dark holes that are neglected. The examination of tunnels is not a pleasant process, and the lights used are rarely too brilliant.[24]

Board of Trade Accident Report on the Tunnel Collapse and Subsequent Derailment of a Pilot Engine at Bramhope Tunnel in 1854, by Col W. Yolland, 2 October 1854

The circumstances connected with the accident are as follows: A pick-up train on the Leeds Northern, consisting of one engine and tender, four passenger carriages, one brake van, five passenger carriages, one brake van, and one passenger carriage, left Arthington station, 9¼ miles from Leeds, for Leeds at 9.30 a.m. on the 19th ultimo, preceded and assisted as usual by a pilot engine (which had safely passed down the tunnel about half an hour before) up the incline of 1 in 94, and it had got about three fourths of the length of the Bramhope Tunnel, travelling at the rate of about 20 miles an hour, when the pilot engine ran over a large mass of stone and rubbish which had fallen from an opening in the arch of the tunnel across both lines, a portion of the arch itself having given way. The tender also passed over some portion of this rubbish, but the engine was thrown off the rails and came suddenly to rest. The front wheels of the second engine mounted this rubbish and the tender of the pilot engine remained suspended by the hook in front of this engine. The collision appears to have been very violent, as the hinder crossbeam below the foot plate, and the foot plate itself of the pilot engine were broken. The guards in front were knocked off, the hand railing considerably damaged, and the chimney knocked off and lay at its side.

The above was a professional assessment of the event; extracts from the *Newry Telegraph* give the human side of the story:

> When the train had proceeded half-way through the tunnel the first engine dashed into a large mass of stones and rubbish lying across the rails [roof had fallen in], and so powerful were the engines that both of the engines and one of the tenders ran over a great quantity of this rubbish …
>
> The shock of the collision drove the passengers against the side and ends of the carriages and against each other with great violence inflicting cuts and bruises and more serious injury upon many. The driver of the first engine, John Graham, was severely crushed in the back and loins, but the other driver and both stockers escaped comparatively uninjured.
>
> Thomas Porrit, the guard, sustained such wounds that doubt is entertained of his recover.
>
> The shock caused the coupling chains of the fifth and sixth carriages to break and the five hindmost carriages, with the guard's van began to descend the decline at Arthington at great speed. Porrit, however, despite his dreadful injuries, managed to put on the brakes and the carriages were brought up at Arthington Station. Scarcely however, had the carriages began to slacken their pace, and before a single passenger could alight, the truck of Irish reapers, which had also become detached was seen descending the incline with frightful velocity, and bashed into the five carriages with a force so great that the truck was shivered to pieces, and the Irishmen were flung in all directions, fortunately not far enough to fall over the embankment, which is very high at that point. The Irishmen were, many of them, most seriously injured, but none killed.
>
> Immediately upon the collision in the tunnel the drivers and stokers hurried from their engines, and most fortunate it was that they did so, for scarcely were they clear when a large mass of the roofing, and the super-incumbent earth

and loose rocks fell in with a terrific crash, burying engines and tenders beneath …

The most seriously injured were –

Mrs Stirling, Belfast, whose leg was fractured.

Mr Geo. Johnson, corn factor, Billingham, who has sustained very painful internal injuries.

Mrs Butterworth, Burley, whose face is badly cut and contused.

Miss Langton, Bath, who has sustained facial injuries but not of a dangerous nature.

Mr Samuel Pickles, Burley, near Otley.

Mr Martin Langley, Liverpool.

Mr William Bolland, Bradford.

Mr Timothy Clarke, Rochdale.

Mr Frank Bowling, Sligo.

Mr Richard Gothey, Ballinasloe, Ireland.

Thomas Porrit, guard.

John Graham, engine driver.

Three ladies from Manchester one of whom sustained severe internal injuries, and the two others serious gashes in the face.

There were 20 or 30 others whose hurts were confined to more trifling cuts and bruises.[25]

The *Wiltshire Independent* highlights the horrendous extent of the collapse:

> On examining the tunnel it appeared that the stone arch had given way for fifteen of its length by eleven feet in width, and that an immense mass of earth and stones had poured down, nearly filling part of the tunnel. Much more of the arch is cracked and depressed and will have to be removed.[26]

Later in October the *Halifax Courier* informed the public of the re-opening and that 'passenger trains would not run until the tunnel had been tested for a week or two by heavy goods train and engines'. That must have been a relief to those who would be using it. The *Courier* finished with, 'The parties injured by the accident are all convalescent.' It was incredible that there had been no loss of life; some might say it was a miracle, but how could it have happened at all the people and the papers asked:

> The serious question in connection with the affair suggests itself. Was not the depressed state of the arch, and the dangerous condition of the tunnel observed before the accident, which placed so many lives in most imminent danger, occurred. We can scarcely suppose that this heap of ruins would fall without previous and palpable warning.[27]

Cambrian Railway Tunnel – Fatal Accident

The Cardiff and Merthyr Guardian, Friday 1 February 1867

FATAL ACCIDENT IN A WELSH TUNNEL

Late on Monday night a shocking accident occurred in a tunnel in one of the deviation lines of the Cambrian Railway, between Glandovey and Aberdovey … it is about 700 yards in length.

For some time past the men had been carrying out certain alterations in accordance with the directions of the government's inspector of railways. About the centre of the tunnel there is a disused shaft … on completion of the tunnel this was filled up and arched over. A short time since the arch was observed to have given way about fifteen inches and orders were issued that the arch should be taken down and a stronger one erected.

Ten men had reported for work at six o'clock that Monday evening and worked until their meal brake at nine, returning to the tunnel at around ten-thirty. A short time after they resumed work the props which had been

Props that were intended to last a lifetime; they shored up the sides of the tunnels and supported the roofs until a more permanent method was needed. A good timberman was a valued asset working in the tunnel. Experience taught him when and if to prop, thereby not wasting money, manpower or time.

supporting the shaft gave way completely – 'a mass of material, estimated at about 100 tons, fell, burying two of the men and injuring several others'. The men, who could, immediately set to work to extricate the two buried men.

As they worked they heard the voice of Jenkins Evans, a carpenter, 'crying out piteously'. He was calling the men by name, begging them not to give-up on him, urging them on as he believed 'he would be drowned by the water which was up to his chin'.

The men redoubled their energies, and after another hour's hard work, at last got sight of the poor fellow, who was found to be lying on some timbers on his breast and still sensible. Two more hours working brought him out, after having been buried for six or seven hours, and was immediately conveyed to his home close by, and attended by Dr Pughe and Mr Lewis, who were on the spot immediately, after the occurrence of the accident. The poor fellow, however, never rallied and died in about a quarter of an hour … He had recently buried his wife, but leaves two children.

Up to the time our parcel was dispatched, no trace has been discovered of the other man, Richard Morris, who is still under the mass of earth. He leaves a wife and three children. Four other men are seriously injured.

The accident is traceable to the thaw and the late heavy rains.

COLLISION

Collisions were commonplace, almost everyday happenings to all railway companies on nineteenth-century British railways. Poor braking systems, no communication systems, failure to make use of communication appliances and especially human error were all reasons for collisions. They happened everywhere and anywhere along railway lines, and especially in tunnels. They involved every variety and combination of trains: goods trains; goods and passenger trains; just passenger trains; passenger and ballast trains (such as that at Blackheath Tunnel). When collisions happened in tunnels, the common denominator in almost every accident was signal error. As David Porter suggests: 'All too often people are blamed for things going wrong (error, fallibility) when it is actually the case that the system they have been given to operate is badly designed by others and they are just doing their best to make it work in the real world rather than the perfect world envisaged by the designers.'[1]

Signalmen and Signalling
Signalmen carried enormous responsibility; people's lives were in their hands. The job could be physically demanding, especially in a large signal box controlling several intersections; operating the signals and points required strenuous pulling and pushing of heavy levers (one box had seventy-nine separate levers), which left even young men physically exhausted

towards the end of their shift. It could also be mentally challenging, especially when fatigued at the end of a long shift. The signalmen worked long hours; twelve-hour, sometimes even eighteen-hour, shifts were not unheard of, particularly if the company had no relief signalman available. They were expected to turn up for duty, no matter what.

In 1892 signalman John Holmes was found guilty of manslaughter after a fatal accident in his section. He had been awake for the previous thirty-six hours, caring for his seriously sick daughter, walking miles trying to find the local doctor (who was away from home tending to another patient), and comforting his distraught wife; because of all this he had reported to the stationmaster at Otterington declaring himself unfit and unable to work the next night's shift. The stationmaster, however, merely asked his superiors for a relief signalman, without stating the full reason, so no relief signalman was sent. Holmes was required to report for work. He then committed the cardinal sin: he fell asleep at his post, then awoke in a confused and anxious state, made a wrong deduction and accepted an express train, which then hurtled into an almost stationary goods train, killing ten people including the guard, and injuring many more.

To be a signalman you had to work your way up. You had to have a good work record, probably first as a porter; you had to be able to read and write (not all could in those times); and then you had to go to special signal school. After passing an exam at the school trainees went to a signal box to practise alongside an experienced signalman until they were ready to take charge on their own. On the small rural lines signalmen mostly worked alone – it could be a lonely job – but all took great pride in their signal boxes and their jobs. The signalman had to know the schedules, and, in theory, the changes to the schedules, which trains were coming through on time, behind time, or if there were cancellations, and what was happening on his section of the line. He had to carry out the rules and regulations to signal them along the line so there was no danger of a crash:

Signals and signalling started very simply with a signalman who signalled the way was clear, underwent many radical changes over the decades before arriving at the system we have today. (Private collection)

The basic rule of the railway was (and is) that only one train at a time is allowed on each section of track. Signalmen used a telegraph system to send electronic messages to each other with information about the location of trains and their direction of travel. Most of the messages were received as bell codes, with different numbers of rings having separate meanings. Once a signalman had decided that he could safely 'accept' a train into his section he would set the semaphore signal that was visible to the train crew. If the signal was set to 'stop' the train would have to stop until the signal changed.[2]

All this was to ensure safety. It sounds great, but it wasn't without its flaws: it did not have 'flexibility', for when equipment broke down (then one could not just pick up the phone but that did come later), and, more importantly, no allowance had been made for human fallibility – this was especially relevant when companies ran on the five-minute interval system. In modern-day parlance, when one addresses only 'artificial intelligence', i.e. 'the equipment', the framework or protocol is always vulnerable. In the words of Maurig Beynon:

> the interaction between conceptual worlds and the real world is very subtle. Ironically, the practical measures designed to protect against the dangers of a breakdown in the tunnel also generated the conceptual framework that led to the disaster. Drastic colocation of trains is a particularly striking example of embodied inconsistency.

Both these components – inflexibility and human error – were major factors in a notable catastrophe; the Clayton Tunnel accident was such a situation.

Clayton Tunnel – An Accident of a Most Appalling Nature

The awful heart-shaking series of collisions which took place on Sunday, August 25 1861, in the railway tunnel through Clayton Hill. On that day, in that gloomy place, twenty-four persons lost their lives, and one hundred and seventy-five were injured ... nothing of horror was wanting, neither in the magnitude nor in the circumstances of the disaster, which long remained in the memories of those who read, and was impossible ever to be forgotten by those who witnessed it.[3]

Who Was Involved?
London Brighton & South Coast Railway – opened on 21 August 1840. Known affectionately as the Brighton Line, or the Brighton, it worked its line on the time-interval system, i.e. five minutes between train departures. It had a poor reputation for punctuality and the erosion of time intervals between trains

Famous Box Tunnel lithograph by J.C. Bourne showing the magnificent entrance, signalman and impressively large signals. The round disc indicated the line was clear, whilst a 'stop' signal was created when the whole post was turned through 90 degrees, bringing a horizontal bar into view. (Private collection)

BOX TUNNEL
WEST FRONT

was not uncommon (the accident report described this practice as 'habitually disregarded', indicating that it happened here *and* on most railway lines).

Brighton Station – place of departure of the three trains involved.

Brighton Station Assistant Stationmaster Charles Legg – the man who dispatched all three trains, but did not stick to the five-minute rule. He gave erroneous times to the inquiry, which were not accepted.

Portsmouth to London Excursion Train – consisted of engine No. 48, tender and sixteen carriages including two

Clayton Tunnel's magnificent entrance showing the little lookout house at the top. (Courtesy of Adrian Backshall, Network Rail)

brake carriages, one behind the tender and one at the tail of the train. It ran once a fortnight, and was running twenty-three minutes behind schedule, operating under Driver Hackman.

Brighton to London Excursion Train – the Craven Wilson-pattern 2-2-2 No. 126 train consisted of engine, tender and seventeen carriages, including two brakes – one behind the tender and one six carriages from the end of the train. It was a regular Sunday excursion train. Its driver, John Scott, made the wrong decision and took the wrong action.

Brighton to London Parliamentary Train – Wilson-pattern Single, locomotive No. 122 (affectionately known as a 'Jenny') train consisting of engine, tender and twelve carriages – two of which were brakes, one behind the tender and one sixth from the end of the train. The last five carriages were to be dropped at stations along the route. A Parliamentary train was a slow-train as it was required to stop at all stations. It was operated by Driver Gregory.

Train Times

	Specified departure	Stationmaster's claim	Actual departure
1st train	08.05	08.22	08.28
2nd train	08.15	08.27	08.31 (+3 mins)
3rd train	08.30	08.36	08.35 (+4 mins)

Clayton Tunnel – a railway tunnel located in the village of Pyecombe near the village of Clayton, West Sussex, between Hassocks and Preston Park railway stations on the Brighton main line. It is situated 5 miles from Brighton on the main line to London; it is the second tunnel out from Brighton, the longest tunnel on the line, at 1 mile, 2 furlongs and 2 chains long, and a two-track tunnel. It was known previously to be a 'dangerous place' because of collisions, and was the first railway tunnel to be protected by a telegraph protocol designed to prevent two trains being in the tunnel on the same line at once. It was controlled by a block section, worked by a single-needle telegraph and protected by a Whitworth automatic revolving banner signal.

South Signal Box – the nearest signal box to Brighton, operated by Signalman Henry Kellick. It was equipped with a clock, an alarm bell, a single-needle telegraph and a distant signal-only hand wheel, with which to operate a signal 350 yards down the line from the box. There were also red (stop) and white (go) flags for use in an emergency. The telegraph had a dial with three indications: 'train in'; 'train out'; 'is train out?' The Board of Trade inspector did not like this because:

William Gladstone's (then president of the Board of Trade) Railway Regulation Act, 9 August 1844, with all its attendant improvements and protection for the 'poorer classes'. Gladstone's 1*d* per mile workers' trains, which provided seats and protection from the weather, ran at least once a day in each direction, stopping at all stations. It changed the face, and safety, of third-class travel. This cartoon 'Parliamentary Trains' shows graphically just how packed the third-class trains were, because they ran so rarely. (Private collection)

A needle telegraph instrument connects signalmen at the portals of the tunnel, and is used for both lines. A deflection of the needle to the left signifies 'train in', and a deflection to the right, 'train out'. When a train enters the tunnel, the signalman displays Danger and sends 'train in' to the man at the other portal. When this train leaves, 'train out' is returned, and the signal turned to Safety. The signals are momentary, and may be interspersed with conversation or signals relating to a train in the other direction.

This meant that signalmen may have needed to be reliant on memory. Engineer Henry Preece in his paper to the Institute of Civil Engineers argued that 'the block wire should be used for nothing but signalling, and the currents should be continuous, not momentary'.[4]

North Signal Box – operated by Signalman John Brown. It too was equipped with a clock, an alarm bell, a single-needle telegraph, as well as a semaphore signal and a distant (Whitworth's) signal.

Board of Trade – Board of Trade inspector Captain H.W. Tyler, Royal Engineers, carried out the accident investigation and made a thorough and lengthy report. This was the worst rail accident up to that time.

Passengers – 589 passengers were travelling in the last two trains that collided.

Operational Practice Between South and North Signal Boxes – Clayton Tunnel was ahead of the times in terms of safety on the railways. It had, to quote Professor David Slater in his study of the accident, 'defined protocols ... multi-protective layers and ... state-of-the-art protection'.[5] It had operated this system safely for a number of years. This accident shook everyone – the employees, company, passengers and society. Numerous papers called it a catastrophe with many descriptive words before – 'terrible', 'horrific', 'dreadful'. O.S. Nock wrote: 'One can almost hear the same comment being made time after time: "I could not imagine that could ever happen."'

How Did it Happen?

Once again it was human error – an inconsistency, a miscommunication or a misunderstanding – between the signalmen in the boxes at each end of the tunnel, which was compounded by faulty equipment and exacerbated by the second driver and guard not carrying out the usual safety procedures and, most significantly, trains not running to the time schedules.

What Should Have Happened

    a) the telegraphic procedure had *only* three signals:
        1)   train in
        2)   train out
        3)   is train out?

    b) operational sequence from either end should run as follows:

train sees and passes 'all right' signal (for 'go')
train enters tunnel
self-acting signal (by means of a treadle on the line and
    weights on the wire) is tripped to activate red (for stop)
    behind them; an alarm bell rings if this does not happen
signalman A telegraphs signal B 'train in'
train passes through tunnel
train exits tunnel
signalman B telegraphs signalman A 'train out'
signalman A resets signal to 'all right' for next train

What Did *Happen*

The first train enters the tunnel and passes the self-acting switch, which fails to set the signal to red. The alarm bell warns Signalman Kellick.

    He first transmits the code 'train in' to Signalman Brown, then fetches the red flag to warn the next train. He waves the red flag.

The second train arrives too soon, passes the green signal, appears not to see the red flag waved by Kellick and enters the tunnel.

The third train is warned in time and comes to a stop before the tunnel entrance.

Kellick returns to his box and signals Brown 'train in', meaning the second train, but Brown believes this still refers to first train, as it is supposed to be not possible for there to be two trains on the same line in the tunnel, at the same time.

Kellick then signals Brown 'is train out?'.

Brown signal backs 'train out' as the first train pulls away from the tunnel, still not knowing that there is a second train in the tunnel.

Meanwhile, the driver of the second train, who had in fact seen Kellick's red flag as he sped by him, decided to stop halfway down the tunnel. He did not send the guard back out of tunnel to give warning further down the track for other trains but instead started to reverse back to the tunnel mouth to talk to Kellick.

Kellick mistakenly believes 'train out' refers to the second train, waves white flag for 'go' to third train. Third train enters tunnel gathering speed.

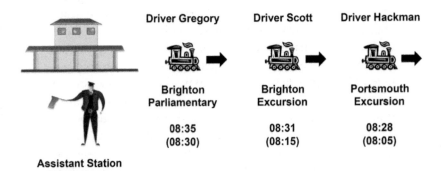

	Driver Gregory	Driver Scott	Driver Hackman
	Brighton Parliamentary	Brighton Excursion	Portsmouth Excursion
	08:35 (08:30)	08:31 (08:15)	08:28 (08:05)

Assistant Station Master Legg

(Courtesy of David Porter)

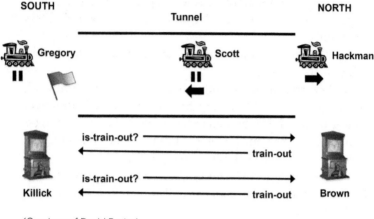

(Courtesy of David Porter)

Third train collides with the second train, which is, against all expectations and procedures, reversing towards it.

What Were the Consequences?

The consequences were awful. The reversing second train and the advancing third train collided with enormous force, propelling the second train forward for some distance down the line, with the third train rearing like a horse on its hind legs, up and over the guard's van and last carriage of the train in front, obliterating them in the action, whilst crushing and killing those inside. (Unfortunately the common practice of leaving the last carriage empty to avoid such happenings had not been enforced here.) This engine kept on going up until its chimney stopped against the tunnel's roof, which is 24ft high. It was fortunate it did not bring the roof down upon them. All this happened despite the fact that Driver Gregory (of the third train), having glimpsed the tail lights of the train in front coming towards him, shut off his steam and threw his engine into reverse, whilst the fireman put the tender brake on; had they not done so the outcome would have undoubtedly been even more dreadful.

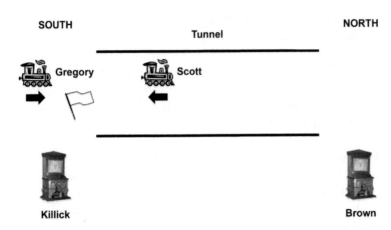

(Courtesy of David Porter)

Freeman's Journal, Tuesday 27 August 1861

The tunnel was quite dark. In a moment it was blocked up with a terrible mass; in which were mingled dead and dying men, women and children buried beneath and amidst heaps of broken carriages, with the engine and tender crowning, and pressing down the whole. To add to the sufferings of the unfortunates, the steam and boiling water descended in showers upon them, scalding those whose bodies were at all exposed.

The feelings of those who first entered the tunnel were harrowed to the last degree.

Many of those who died were in the 'terrible mess' of this last carriage, where passengers were crushed, burnt or scalded to death. The flimsy, open-sided carriages of the excursion train may actually have saved lives as many passengers were 'thrown out into the tunnel rather than being killed in their seats'.[6] 'On the wreck being removed it was found that eight men, eleven women and three children were killed – twenty-two in all. The corpses were so disfigured and blackened that it was difficult to distinguish whether they were male or female.' [7]

Edward Charlwood, naturalist/travelling bird-seller, 101 London Road, Brighton. He left a son about 12 years of age who accompanied Cecilia Gibbons when she made her sworn testimony to identify his father.

George Gardner, cab proprietor, aged 38, identified by his brother. His wife Emma Gardner later brought a case against the LB&SC rail company for negligence that 'occasioned her husband's death', and was awarded £500. Hers was the first trial of many.

John Greenfield, an apprentice, aged 17. He was visiting Mr Greenfield, a greengrocer, at 5 Montpelier Place, Brighton; identified by Frederick Nell.

John Lockstone, income tax assessor and collector, aged about 50, 32 Adelphi Terrace, Victoria Park, London; identified by William Bartlett.

John Ingledew Snr, baker, 78 St James's Street, Brighton; identified by his son-in-law, Thomas Parker Durrant, an auctioneer.

William Hubbard, labourer in Victoria Docks, and his grandson, **Henry Howard Hubbard**, aged 4. They had been staying at 17 Viaduct Terrace; identified by Fanny Clark, of the same address.

John Wheeler, cellar man to Mr Willis, a wine merchant, aged 46, his wife **Elizabeth Wheeler**, aged 46, and their 18-month-old son, **Daniel Wheeler**, all of 24 London Street, Brighton. They left nine other children. They were identified by their son John Wheeler, aged 24.

Catherine Barnard, wife of a shoemaker, aged 70 or 71 according to her husband, 22 Charles Street, Brighton; identified by her husband.

Christiana Manthorpe, shopwoman at Mr Trill's Embroidery Shop on the corner of Duke Street and West Street, aged 34, residing at Lennox Arms, 13 Richmond Street, Brighton; identified by John Storey the publican.

Ellen Lower, wife of a bricklayer, aged 47 or 48 (her husband was not sure), 1 Liverpool Street, Brighton. She was identified by her husband who had been on the train with her and their two boys. They were in the first excursion train sitting together with their back to the engine, one boy beside them and one facing them. Her husband told the court there were nine in the compartment – his family, another man and his wife, two more females and an elderly gentleman. He told the court that when they stopped, 'his boy was looking out of the window, he saw the guard's door open and another train was coming. Just as he said that, there came a concussion all at once.'

Coroner: 'In what state was the carriage in which you were sitting?'

'It was smashed all to atoms from behind.'

Coroner: 'Where did you find yourself?'

'At the top of the ruins.'

Coroner: 'Did you discover your wife after?'

'Yes she was under the ruins, under a heavy weight and I saw that she was quite dead. I pulled two out of the ruins before I extricated my wife. I got her head out and nursed it until she went cold. I don't think she felt anything.'

Jane Elizabeth Biden, aged 24, of 5 Matilda Street, Islington, London, and **Elizabeth Wright** of same address. They had been in Brighton a week. Jane was identified by her poor mother, Mary Temple of Sussex Street, Cliftonville, whilst

Elizabeth was the last to be identified at the commencement of the inquest, by Eliza Diaper, of the same address.

Maria Edwing, visitor, was travelling with her daughter Elizabeth, aged 2, who was seriously injured, badly scalded and both legs fractured. Elizabeth stayed in hospital a number of weeks; identified by her husband.

Rebecca Barclay, milliner, aged about 30, from London, had been staying with a Mr William Biggs in Brighton; he identified her body.

Mary Gillett, widow, aged 68, visitor at 29 Upper Gardener Street, Brighton; resided at Weaver's Almshouses, Wantage; identified by Edward Coomber, who lived at the address where she had been staying.

Mary Parker, wife of Thomas Parker, bricklayer (injured and lying in hospital), aged about 50, 25 Upper James's Street, Brighton; identified by Richard Thomas Monkford.

Agnes Parker, aged 16, resided at 35 Oriental Place, Brighton, with her aunt who ran a lodging house. **Mary Ann Parker**, aged 11, lived with her father of 8 Phillip Street, Kingsland Road; identified by Mary Ann Beard, who told the court: 'She had been down for a holiday. They have no mother but a father, who is here but is not in a fit state to come and give evidence.'

George Wescott, a boy aged 12, of Old St Pancras Road, London, was staying at 44 Lewes Street, Brighton; identified by John Bailey who had been sitting next to the boy in the train carriage. When asked by the court what the boy's trade was, he answered that he 'was only twelve'.

Another died later whilst in hospital: **Anthony Kean**, saster tailor, aged 64, making a **total of twenty-three persons**

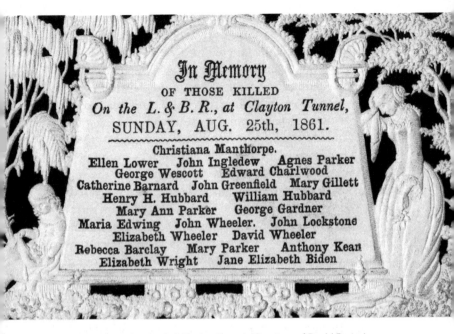

Memorial card to the dead of Clayton Tunnel. (Courtesy of David Porter)

who lost their life. Some of the local victims were buried in the Extra-Mural Cemetery, Brighton.

Around 176 were hurt to a lesser or greater degree – some with life-changing injuries. These included lacerations, splinters – small, and large (remember the coaches would have been made of wood which becomes spear-like when splintered), contusions, internal injuries, broken limbs, fractures to arms and legs, severe scalding and severe shock. Several were conveyed to hospital for treatment, where they remained for weeks – like Mr Pegg of the Royal Oak Hotel who had compound fractures to both legs. 'One woman,' it was reported, 'had her scalp torn completely off ... the injuries in other cases are too shocking for description.'[8] One particularly unusual happening and injury was reported:

'Mr Parsons, 32, was sitting opposite a man who was eating with a knife, when the force of the collision caused the man to fall forward, the knife entered into the jaw of Mr Parsons, inflicting a severe wound.'[9]

The first part of the front train suffered little from this mighty impact; it was, in fact, quite undamaged. The passengers were shaken from their seats and onto each other but not greatly hurt. Their fear, however, was great. As one passenger described it: 'The yells and shrieks of the people were awful, not only those who were injured but the rest of the passengers of the two trains, whose alarm, increased by the darkness, was intense. People were distracted with terror.'[10] This front portion was, after some time, detached from the damaged part and went onto Hassock Gate station where all received assistance. As soon as was possible, the wounded, the dead and the dying were conveyed to Brighton; it took a long time to extricate the rest – people, train parts and engine. The dead were taken to the Reading Room of the Railway Literary Institution where they were laid out on tables and forms, covered in sheets, awaiting identification. The news had travelled fast and the Reading Room was soon besieged by anxious people. The wounded were taken in carriages and flys to Sussex County Hospital.[11]

Board of Trade Report, 5 October 1861

Principal cause was 'the inefficiency of the system under which the traffic was worked between Brighton and Hassock Gate'.

1   Only one telegraph-needle was used for signalling the trains on both lines of rails through Clayton Tunnel – makes it easy for signalmen make a mistake or to misunderstand each other.
2   Neither signalmen had record books which would have helped them see the problem as they recorded the trains.

[Also all those who needed to know the time took their time from different uncoordinated clocks.]

3   The trains ran at 'intervals of time' rather than 'intervals of space' [i.e. the block-system] – time is easily eroded or overlooked.

Secondary causes that contributed to the accident:

1   Mistake made by Signalman Brown in reporting 'train is out' [he believed it to refer to the first train].
2   Signalman Kellick's hastily repeated question 'is train out?' [regarding second train] causing confusion for Brown.
3   Kellick admitting third train after he had shown red flag to second train [he believed tunnel was empty as Brown had reported train is out].
4   Driver John Scott contributed to the accident 'by mistake and not carelessly' by reversing his train back down the track [although this was against company procedure].
5   The absence of a break [brake] van at the tail of the third train; with five passengers carriages behind it [they were to be 'dropped' at different stations on the way] it did not exert enough braking pressure and so did not slow the train as much as it could have, had it been at the end of the train.
6   It was disgraceful that a man in so responsible a position as Signalman Kellick should be compelled to work for twenty-four hours at a stretch in order to earn one day of rest a week [tiredness affecting his ability and judgements]. In fairness to the company this was Kellick's own choice and practice, rather than working the usual eighteen-hour shift, but it should not have been necessary or allowed.

Coroner's Court

A nine-day inquest into the twenty-three deaths was conducted by David Black, Esq., the borough coroner. Local tradesmen, as was the usual practice, were sworn in for jury duty – in this instance there were fifteen. No one who had a commercial interest in or relationship to the case could be called (many locals had business dealings with the railway company).

Mr Joseph Watts Heming, grocer, Bartholomew, (?), foreman
Daniel Harding Greenin, toy dealer, East Street
Mr William Tozer, boot and shoemaker, 1 New Road
Mr Henry Potter, auctioneer, 155 North Street
Mr William Johnson, hotelkeeper, Clarence Hotel
Mr John Holder, china and glass man, Black Lion Street
Mr John Charles Cochrane, grocer, North Street
Mr Charles Court, toy dealer, North Street
Mr Frederick Willard, tailor, 2 Western Road
Mr Thomas Francis, grocer, 74 Western Road
Mr Henry Cadell Gould, juvenile clothier, 71 Western Road
Mr Alfred Wood, upholsterer, 36 Western Road
Mr William Stanford, cheesemonger, 24 Prince Albert Street
Mr William Merry, wine merchant, 34 King's Road
Mr Edward Geer, hotelkeeper, White Horse Hill

The court was initially held up by the company's reluctance to release statements given to them by their employees involved in the case, citing the fact that they contained 'privileged and confidential information'.

These documents included:

a) A report made by Driver Scott, the driver of the excursion train from Brighton to London on Sunday 25 August detailing the circumstances of the accident
b) Scott's daily returns
c) The verbal statement of W. Boynett, head guard of the train, taken down in writing by Turner, one of the clerks in Superintendent Craven's office
d) A statement made by Butcher, the guard
e) The report made by Driver Hackman, the driver of the Portsmouth excursion, handed to Vaughan, the officer at the Brighton Station

These documents obviously had great bearing on the case, and eventually the company agreed to release them 'to assist the inquiry'. When the inquiry eventually got under way it turned into something of a schoolboy spat event with the two signalmen accusing and counter-accusing each other.

'I did – he didn't', 'He did – I didn't', an 'unseemly wrangle'. Meanwhile, Assistant Stationmaster Legg set up a smokescreen around the times of departures of the trains, talking of different clocks and watches, and the LB&SC's Railway Superintendent John Chester Craven robustly defended the Department of Traffic – arguing fiercely (almost to the point of perjury one could say) that the reversing of a train was within company practice, when it was absolutely not. Overall it appeared that Kellick was to be the sacrificial lamb; the jury, however, thought differently.

The Jury's Verdict
Despite all of the above, the jury did not find any negligence by either of the signalmen, Kellick or Brown, but they judged Assistant Stationmaster Legg to have acted recklessly in dispatching the trains too close together and against the time rules of the company and, therefore, 'by his negligence and want of caution, did in an essential degree contribute to and indirectly cause the deaths of the persons so killed'.[12]

He was charged with manslaughter and was committed for trial. He appeared at Lewes Assizes, but it was found there was no true bill against him, and he was not tried. So, in effect, it was nobody's fault.

Board of Trade Recommendation
'The adoption of absolute block working [i.e. along the whole line] and continuous brakes on the trains.'

The railway did nothing about the recommendation at this time. Superintendent Craven wrote in reply: 'My board feel bound to state frankly that they have not seen reason to alter the views which they have so long entertained on this subject, and they still fear that the telegraphic system of working recommended by the Board of Trade will, by transferring much responsibility from the engine driver, augment rather than diminish the risk of accident.'

One effect the accident did have was to halt Sunday excursions temporarily – much to the chagrin of George F. Chambers, a 'keep Sabbath sacred' advocate, who later wrote, in *Eastbourne Memories of the Victorian Period 1845 –1901*, 'It put a stopper on Sabbath-breaking excursioning for a long time: would it had done so permanently!'[13]

The disaster was a high price to pay for things not meeting expectations. David Porter concludes in his paper, 'Persistent Analogue Threats: Fallible Humans and Resonating Systems', that:

> The Clayton Tunnel disaster was an example of people doing their best to make a system work but ultimately being defeated by tiredness, poor judgement, mechanical breakdown and the blind faith of the system's designers in a clockwork world where the unimaginable could never happen.[14]

Blackheath Tunnel – Two Trains Wrecked

This 'frightful accident' was the result of a collision between the 2.40 p.m. express passenger train from Maidstone and a ballast train, carrying workmen, which took place in the Blackheath Tunnel on the North Kent Railway, on the evening of Friday 16 December 1864.

Primary cause:	signaller error
Secondary causes:	excessive train load, station staff error
Result:	rear collision
Outcome:	6 fatalities, 19 injured

The heavily laden ballast train of several trucks had struggled to gather speed and momentum up the rising gradient of 168, on wet rails, after its stop at Charlton. It managed to get partially through the tunnel when, 'from some cause or other', the last six trucks, which contained several platelayers and labourers, became disconnected, and whilst the front of the train continued on, seemingly unaware, they stopped still. Dead still. The equally heavy express train, which left Maidstone around 2.20 p.m., consisted of an engine and tender and fifteen vehicles, of which two were brake carriages, and one was a brake van. Having seen the signals set to 'all right', the driver drove the train into the tunnel at a good speed of 30mph and smashed into the standing trucks. It was a violent collision which threw the men and the ballast trucks around and crushed them 'one upon the other' so all ended up mangled and broken. The engine and the tender were thrown on their sides as were the first two carriages, which were 'shivered to pieces', an oft-used expression to say they were 'in bits'. It all totally blocked the tunnel. The shrieks and cries from the frightened and the injured could be heard coming out of the tunnel at the Charlton end. It was investigated, and then all other traffic was stopped from either end.

Officials and workmen hastily made their way to the tunnel from both ends; what they saw was a horrible sight. Five of the labourers were already dead beneath the trucks. The driver and fireman were underneath the engine, badly scalded. From the almost destroyed front carriages 'no less than eight males and six female persons were removed, very much injured ... A large number of passengers, who were only shaken or contused, were rescued from all descriptions of perilous positions.'[15]

A correspondent of *The Times* happened to be a passenger on the train, and later recounted his ghastly personal experience in print:

> The signal was given that the tunnel was clear. I know that we were going a great rate, and that no check whistle or

any other indication was given, but at the speed of 35 or 40 miles an hour, we rushed onto something apparently solid, and then the horrid sound of everything in front crushing down before out carriage, which was rushing on over broken carriages, sleepers etc., and now 4 or 5 feet in the air, then dashing sideways, then partially recovering its perpendicular, as it struck against the side of the tunnel.

This, of course, is the work of seconds, but oh! those seconds to us. At last came one violent crash, and then the rest and total silence for one second, while each one seemed to draw in deep breath, – but for one second only; and then the sounds. I have often heard the shrieks of the timid, but never before the groans of the severely injured. God grant I may never again. I feel as if they could never leave me, and when in a few minutes later I got out of the carriage and went to the mass of bruised, dying, crippled, bleeding creatures, I feel too, this sight is riveted on my vision, for ever. I dare not try to close my eyes on it – it become more distinct. Perhaps the most anxious moment, personally, was the moment when I found I was not seriously injured, but about to die of suffocation.

The whole tunnel was full of steam and sulphurous vapour, and had it lasted many moments more, the wounded and those who had no wounds, would have slept together. But it decreased, and we lived.

The next most dreadful moment was when we could hear the down-train coming, and such a shriek arose from all as only despair could raise. For fifteen minutes no guard or anyone in authority came near us. The only light we had was from the carriages and held by passengers but so embedded were the poor sufferers, that they could only be assisted by giving them more pain, the splinters sticking into them in every part. Four young gentlemen, they were officers I believe, *behaved admirably*. They were in the front compartment of my carriage. When the shock came they were all thrown together, and when they attempted to get up, the carriage, to the level of the window, was filled with the tops and sides of the two covered third-class carriages. They had not room even to sit up. How they had escaped being beheaded I cannot make out. They crawled out and came to my compartment, and as they climbed up, without hats – hair, face hands all bloody and black, I thought they came to die, but after a few minutes (although seriously hurt they had no bones broken), they were the most efficient assistants to those more seriously injured, and God bless them, they behaved very well.

It was about one hour-and-a-half before the wounded and dead were removed. After that we packed ourselves where we could. The carriage I had travelled in being off the rails and much broken, was left behind. Slowly we moved back to Charlton.

On enquiring at the hinder part of the train, I found that what had crushed all my front to splinters, had only been felt as a rude stoppage behind, and hardly disturbed them at all.[16]

Persons Killed at the Time of the Accident
Servants of the Company – All in the Ballast Train
William Wade   a platelayer, residing at New Cross
William Jones   a labourer, of Lewisham
William Morris a labourer, living in the Old Kent Road
Henry Smith   a labourer, address not known
William Seeley a labourer, address not known

Persons Who Died Later of Injuries Sustained in the Accident
Edward Allum   fireman of the up passenger train from Maidstone resided at Peckham. Very severely scalded around face and neck. Died at 12 a.m. at Woolwich Marine Hospital, where he had been taken
Edward Cullin   died at Woolwich Marine Hospital
Joseph Hunt   driver, died at Antigallican, Charlton[17]

Coroner's Court

The inquest was opened on Tuesday 20 December 1864 and was still on going through January until early February 1865; it had to be reconvened several times to accommodate those who died at intervals after the event and to allow the recovery of the injured. Indeed, one of the sittings took place in the hospital where Thomas Randal, the brakeman of the ballast train, was recovering. When he was told that 'with the exception of two platelayers in this train you are the only person who has escaped', he replied 'I am aware of that and I thank God I am alive.'

One that survived was William Henry Lancaster, the guard, and it was obvious that there was a belief, by the coroner at least, that he had not carried out his duties in making 'a warning for other trains'. Under strong questioning from the coroner (who obviously believed that there was something 'going on' as he asked whether Randal had been asked 'to hold his tongue' by Lancaster when he had visited him in hospital – twice), Randal confirmed that the last truck had lamps that were lit; he did not know that the train was to split; and someone, but he did not know who because there was much fog and much smoke in the tunnel so could not see had said 'put your brake on Tom' and he had put it on and kept it on because he could feel the train going back. When asked again, he said he had put the brake on 'as soon as the signal was given' and that no one had got out and come to talk to him or asked 'for a Lucifer or a light'; he was just about to get down from the truck to see what was going on when it was struck.[18]

Canonbury Tunnel – 'Not One, Not Two, Not Even Three, but Four … and Nearly Five … Trains in a Tunnel!'

'The whole matter turns on a misinterpretation of signals received by the Great Northern signalman at Canonbury,'

writes the *Railway Review* in December 1881, a few days after
the accident:

> The signalman at Finsbury Park who was so busy sending
> train after train to death and destruction into the tunnel
> was neither drunk nor insane. He had not been taken ill.
> He was not fatigued. Unhappily, as a real relief signalman, he
> had confused the bell code messages from Canonbury (a box
> under the auspices of the North London Company) and had
> interpreted the code 'line blocked' as 'train able to proceed
> under caution' ...

The 8.35 a.m. train from Finchley [1] which had left
Finsbury Park bound for Broad Street on the newly opened
section of line was stopped by signals at the south end of
Canonbury tunnel. It was a minute before nine o'clock on
a snowy 10th December. Three or four minutes later this
Finchley train was knocked forward slightly by a crash in
the rear. Delighted at the break from the daily monotony,
a number of passengers eagerly clambered out of the train
to find that the 8.58 a.m. from Finsbury Park [2] had run
into the rear. They were ordered into the train by the driver
who had received cautionary permission to proceed into
Canonbury. The Finchley train arrived there without damage
giving its passengers a lively morning talking point.

Unhappily the incidents were only just beginning. The
standing 8.58 a.m. from Finsbury Park was struck violently
in the rear by the 8.43 a.m. from Enfield [3]. Hardly had
some of the passengers alighted from the Enfield train
under the escort of a guard and crossed to the other side
of the tunnel when a fourth train approached. In spite of
the efforts of this guard the fourth train crashed with great
impetus into the third train. The engine and carriages reared
up and crashed against the walls of the tunnel. The guard,
Harry Catherall, ran back the 500 yards to Finsbury Park
signal box and was in time to stop a fifth train from entering
the tunnel under clear signals.[19]

The passengers who were killed were in the two rear carriages of the third train. There is no question from the serious nature of their injuries that death was instantaneous.

Mr Joseph Henry Newman, of 51 Victoria-street Finsbury-park, solicitor's clerk, age 25.
Mr G. Ament, 155 Leadenhall Street, a German about 40.
Mr E.W. Saunders 1 Devon-villas, Palmerston-road, Bowes – park, age 23.
Alexander Vickery, cowkeeper, Mild-may road, Stoke Newington, age 73.
William West, a passenger-guard in the service of the North London Railway Company.[20]

Once again many, believed to be well over 100, were injured.

A great many claims for compensation were brought against the Great Northern over several years after the accident. An interesting one was that of Mrs Frances Eliza West, widow of the passenger guard, and her two stepchildren aged 13 and 10 years, who brought an action against the company under the Employer's Liability Act. The company 'consented a verdict of £500. The Judge directed that £400 be paid to the widow and £100 to be held in trust for the children.'[21] There were others with much higher amounts such as:

Manchester Courier and Lancashire General Advertiser, Saturday 18 November 1882
HEAVY DAMAGES AGAINST RAILWAY COMPANY
In the Queen's Bench Division on Tuesday an article clerk named Jellicoe obtained £750 damages from the Great Northern Railway for injuries sustained in accident in Canonbury Tunnel last December.

There were others of substantial amounts for the time, such as Hodgson, a ship broker, who received £1,300 in May 1883.

In May 1884 the Great Northern discharged:

1,000 to 1,200 men, including 300 in the London district. These were mostly bricklayers, carpenters, joiners other artisans and labourers. At the same time their clerks had a reduction of ten percent ... It is stated that the very high damages entailed upon the company by the collisions in Canonbury Tunnel and at Hornsey Station, have rendered a reduction in expenses inevitable.[22]

Still, their pain was not over – the worst was yet to come. The most startling amount of all was that awarded to Gerhard, a businessman and colour merchant. It had obviously been fiercely contested for the length of time it took to reach settlement:

Dundee Evening Telegraph, Thursday 16 July 1885

At the Middlesex Sheriff's Court, in the case of Gerhard v Great Northern Railway £4,000 damages were award to the plaintiff for severe personal injuries received in the collision in Canonbury Tunnel on 19 December 1881.

The Jury's Verdict

The jury attributed the accident to 'the unauthorised mode of working introduced by signalman Holey' and made recommendations for 'the better working of the railway in question'.[23]

Board of Trade Recommendation

Inspector Colonel Yolland recommended 'that the permissive block should be struck off the North London instructions, and that speaking telegraphic instruments be supplied to each signal box'.

The 'permissive block' allows more than one train at a time to be on the same line in a block section or a signal section, which means that trains are permitted to pass signals indicating the line ahead is occupied, but only at such a speed that they can safely drive by sight. There were also standard procedures for trains driving forward: proceed with caution and keep sufficient distance from the train in front to prevent the second train colliding with first in case of an emergency stop.

The permissive block was not actually part of the operations of the Great Northern, but, for some reason, was still in the working codebook, and it had been taken up by the signalman – with the devastating consequence.

Frodsham Tunnel – A Dreadful Railway Accident

'Several fatal accidents, and one of a peculiarly distressing nature, have again directed attention to the insufficient guarantees for public safety existing in the management of Railway Companies,' writes *The Household Narrative of Current Events* in 1851. 'If any writer of fiction had imagined such an incident as that of the Frodsham Tunnel, on the Chester Junction Railway, it would at once have been condemned as too monstrous to be credible.'

'Dreadful Railway Accident,' said the heading of *The Times* report of Friday 2 May 1851, a masterpiece of understatement. It involved three trains, some 1,500 people of whom upwards of thirty-five were badly or seriously injured, unknown large numbers of people hurt, and eight persons killed – five in the darkness of the tunnel and three dying later of their injuries.

Wednesday 30 April was the principle race day of Chester races. The three trains passing through the tunnel were carrying race-goers back to Manchester and Warrington. The trains were long and jam-packed full, and, in the case of the first train, too long and too full, with an engine that was too weak to pull the load. It ground to a halt and the others collided into it and each other. Considering the numbers of trains and people involved, it could have been a lot worse.

EXPLOSION

And a Short History of Explosives

Blasting was often a necessary and vital part in the creation of tunnels; without it the work would have been impossible or taken an inordinate amount of time that would seriously impact on the costs. Many of the materials used in and during the work were highly volatile and unreliable, as well as having dangerous smoke and vapours. The use of explosive and highly flammable materials in a confined space increased the danger level of this workplace. Added to that, the fact that for most of the time the men could not withdraw out of the tunnel before the explosions took place increased the danger level further, from a probable nine to more like ten plus. Mix in with that a workforce that was not adverse to risk-taking and the whole situation could truly be described as an accident waiting to happen.

All kinds of explosives were used in blasting at that time: gunpowder; guncotton; dynamite; gelignite/gelatin; tonite; compressed powder; pebble powder; naptha.

Powder made so much smoke as to be objectionable and was not strong enough for hard rock, whilst the fumes of dynamite and naptha were extremely deleterious to health and so dangerous in another way.

Gelignite or blasting gelatin was one of the cheapest explosives (making it attractive to contractors). It burns slowly and cannot explode without a detonator, so it can be stored safely. It proved best in hard rock, so was popular for tunnel-makers;

an experienced miner could blast a hole exactly, but in the 1880s the Board of Trade required the makers to suspend manufacture and return all material to store.[1]

Tonite, an equal mixture of guncotton and a nitrate, or sometimes a nitro-compound was popular in the later decades. According to Thomas Walker, a Severn Tunnel contractor, nearly all the work in the Severn Tunnel was done by tonite (although an article written up in a local paper spoke specifically about the use of dynamite in that tunnel). Tonite is a carefully prepared explosive made into handy packages which the miners called 'pills' (still known as pills in the quarry industry today) with a detonator attached to some of the cartridges, which were then known as primers. Primers are detonator sensitive and act as an explosive amplifier, initiating non-detonator-sensitive explosives – dynamite would act as a primer as it is detonator sensitive.

The fuse was attached to the primer, and then, according to the depth of the hole and the strength of the material to be blasted, a primer, and between one and four pills were placed in the hole. Very little tamping was required. Tonite was not damaged by water nor did it seem affected by cold as dynamite was, and the fumes were so slight that it was possible to return to the face within a minute of the blast; however, Tonite had a relatively low detonation velocity and hence low detonation pressure, and so was not always strong enough for the job and would sometimes leave a 'socket' – a short length of hole at the bottom where the explosive had not broken the rock.[2] The higher the detonation pressure, the better the shockwave going into the rock to break up its structure before the gas pushes the broken rock out.

Again in the Severn Tunnel, but much less frequently, cartridges of compressed lime were also tried. These work by first drilling a large borehole, which is then filled with the cartridges, but then instead of a fuse a tube is placed at the top of the cartridges, and when the tamping has been placed, water is pushed by a force-pump through the tube onto the cartridges, causing the swelling of the lime and the release of gas to displace the rock. They were found to be not very effective; mostly the lime just blew out its tamping but displaced no rock. This situation caused a bad accident to the foreman, Joseph Talbot, when the tamping and a quantity of lime flew out straight into his eyes, after one of the holes was loaded and the water pumped in. It was feared he would lose his sight, but happily it recovered after a couple of days.[3]

Naptha and naphtha vapour were both fire and explosion hazards. Naphtha is a general term that has been used to refer to mixtures of highly volatile and flammable liquid hydrocarbon. Each such mixture is obtained during the distillation of different materials – coal tar, occasionally wood and, in later times, petroleum. Accordingly, it is known by its parent name, such as coal-tar naphtha, or wood naphtha, petroleum naphtha or just naphtha.

Shepton Mallet Journal, Friday 19 October 1883

EXPLOSIONS IN A TUNNEL

THE INNER CIRCLE RAILWAY

In connection with the work in progress for the completion of the Inner Circle Tunnel two fires accompanied by explosions occurred on Thursday. Official Report:

About four hundred gallons of naptha was destroyed and a quantity of loose wood was severely damaged by fire in the tunnel. A number of workmen are engaged day and night and at the early fire the escape of those present was surprising. 'Spirit upset' is supposed to be the cause. The firemen had not proceeded four yards before the force of an explosion caused a hasty retreat, and another explosion followed placing the men in great danger. The suffocating fumes also much retarded the members of the brigade in their work. In the afternoon the brigade were summoned to the same scene the outbreak being occasioned by the 'vapour of naptha coming in contact with a lighted lamp'.

The fireman again had a troublesome task. Henry Baker aged 42, and George Sharp aged 24, engaged on the works were seriously burned about the hands and face.

Gunpowder, sometimes known as the accident that changed the world, has been around for centuries: some say since as early as the ninth century, originating in China when an alchemist was looking for a life-enhancing elixir but instead found a flammable powder. It was a mixture of saltpetre, sulphur and charcoal; the latter darkened it into 'black powder' and thereby gave it its common usage name. Originally used for warfare, and, latterly, for entertainment as pyrotechnics (fireworks), it is believed it was eventually used in mining as early as the fifteenth century. Up to that time hard rock had to be broken by hard labour, or, sometimes, by setting wood fires and heating the rock to red-hot before pouring on cold water to cool it as quickly as possible and thereby causing it to 'crack'. Black-powder explosions are not a detonation (velocity of the reaction is below the speed of sound in the material) so does not have a detonation shock wave to crack the rock; rather it is the expanding gas that breaks up the rock. Very hard rock such as granite would be very difficult to blast with black powder, although it is good for taking out large lumps, such as for a sculptor. Gunpowder could also be formed into shapes to meet a requirement.

Wickwar Tunnel – Gunpowder Accident

Wickwar Tunnel, some 14 miles from the small town of the same name, lay on the Bristol & Gloucestershire Railway. It was being blasted through hard limestone rock, which required large amounts of explosives each day – some 10–16lbs of powder every twelve hours. Shaft No. 5 of this tunnel was to become the scene of a most 'lamentable occurrence' – awful in nature and in consequence – but which could still have been much worse.

For the convenience of the workmen a small blacksmith shop had been constructed close by this shaft. Here the men could easily have broken tools repaired, and, even more conveniently, for those coming off shift out of the tunnel (or pit as it was sometimes called before it truly became a tunnel) they could go to dry their clothes (tunnels were always wet, sodden places to a lesser or greater degree) so a warm fire nearby on a cold winter's night was very handy and welcome.

It was Friday evening, and also Christmas Eve. There would be no working the next day, or the day after, so the explosive would not be needed until Monday morning. The blacksmith's fire was drawn, everyone was anxious to get off home and it was decided it would be fine to leave the barrel containing 100lbs of gunpowder and another, on top, with 6lbs of loose powder – this was open but covered with a mackintosh inside – maybe 12ft from the forge, but only 4ft from the anvil of the blacksmith's conveniently close workshop. The scene was set: a disaster waiting to happen. The banksman (Jones) who had placed the powder in the shed, as per usual, had been specifically instructed to make sure to move it out and away *before* the blacksmith fired up for work on the Monday morning. Maybe Jones had had a good holiday and slept a little late, or maybe the blacksmith was eager to get on after his break, but before the man could remove the barrels, the blacksmith had lit his fire and set to work 'hammering his hot irons on the anvil, with sparks flying in all directions' just yards away from this immense mass of dangerous materials.

The inevitable happened. The waiting disaster struck! A tremendous explosion woke and shook the whole town of Wickwar from their beds at 7 a.m. that disastrous Monday morning, on 27 December 1841; the shock could be felt for miles. Windows in many of the Wickwar houses were blown in or out, but that was the least of the mischief. Realising where the explosion had come from, hundreds left their homes and came to see what had happened, and to help.

The spectacle that presented itself was pitiable in the extreme. The building was completely levelled to the ground, and fragments of stone and timber were strewn about in all directions. About 80 yards from the spot where the shed had stood was the body of Jones, the man who had placed the powder in the hut and who, it is conjectured, was in the act of removing it when the explosion occurred. He had been thrown through the roof of the shed, to a height of 20 yards, and fell at the distances as stated, looking, as a witness described, like 'a mass of black rags'. In another direction the unhappy blacksmith was seen running at top speed, his clothes ablaze, and himself scorched and smutted. Six other men lay stretched on the ground dreadfully injured.

There were eight people inside the shed when the explosion occurred; two died instantly; one, James Bennet, lasted a couple of hours after suffering such excruciating pain that he had asked them to 'knock him on his head and end his misery'; and the five others who were 'horribly wounded' were conveyed first to the New Inn at Wickwar and later to the Bristol Infirmary.

The dead at the scene were: Matthew Stephens (26) miner in Shaft No. 5, James Jones (27) banksman – both single and both so hideously burned and shattered, they presented a 'sickening sight' – and James Bennet (29) miner, married, with a heavily pregnant wife expecting their first child.

Those taken to the infirmary were: Thomas White, Lewis Crew, George Collins, John Hodge and Henry Williams, the blacksmith, who died later.

These men all worked under a Mr John Stephens, a miner from Cornwall, and second cousin to Matthew Stephens. He identified all the deceased and injured – he had seen at close hand their demise, having been in the shed just a few minutes beforehand and was just outside collecting horses when it all happened. He told the coroner he had been in 'mining and excavations since infancy' for some thirty-eight years; he was a foreman, a sub-contractor under Mr Brunel for sixteen years, and he had previously worked at Box Tunnel. He also informed the court that:

[W]e had no other place to put the powder. We always put it in there ... have done so since I have been on this pit which is thirteen weeks ... but take it out before the blacksmith begins his work. When the blacksmith is at work the powder is kept out on the bank, and if it rains we throw the skip, or macintosh, or our clothes over it. When the powder is put in the blacksmith's shop it is usual to put planks of wood around it ... When I was employed in Box we had there a little hut to keep the powder in.[4]

The inquest was adjourned in order to allow those injured to recover enough to attend the hearing. Two (unnamed) had been discharged by the Bristol Infirmary and were able to attend (whilst three still remained in). The jury found that whilst the deaths were 'occasioned by the accidental explosion of a large quantity of gunpowder thoughtlessly placed in the blacksmith's shop', they strongly held both John Stephens, the foreman, and James Jones responsible. They both had acted incredibly irresponsibly: Stephens a) by allowing such a large quantity of gunpowder to be around when a smaller quantity was needed each day; and b) by ordering and allowing the powder to be held in such a potentially dangerous place, that is, the blacksmith's. Whilst Jones a) had not informed the blacksmith of the situation of so much gunpowder being so close by; and b) neglected his duty of not turning up before the blacksmith had started work to remove the powder. Thankfully for the memory of Jones, they did not consider his neglect wilful, otherwise they would have had to reach a verdict of manslaughter rather than accidental death. They hoped that this awful accident would 'stimulate those influential people engaged in the work to bring to bear their authority to prevent, as far as possible, a future such accident'.[5]

One interesting and somewhat alarming fact had come to light during the course of the hearings: it had become commonplace for 'individuals [from the works] bringing into town and illegally keeping on their premises [that is the houses in which they were staying] large quantities of gunpowder, seriously endangering the lives and property of the inhabitants' of the town. Presumably this was the powder that still remained in their individual powder tins unused at the end of the day's work. Rather than return it to the store, they took it home! The coroner again strongly requested those employed in superintending the works to act quickly to put a stop to this.

Hose Tunnel – A Matter of Three Candles

The accident at Hose Tunnel is one that makes you shake your head in sheer disbelief.

Everyone who knows of gunpowder knows it is highly flammable and explosive when set alight, so it is best not to have any naked flames near it. Yet the miners at this time worked purely by the light of a naked candle flame – in close proximity to the gunpowder they were working with. If ever there was a disaster waiting to happen, it was this. The only wonder is that it did not happen more often.

One hears a lot about the cavalier attitude to safety and the high level of risk-taking of the navvies, but, as often pointed out by the railway inspectors, there was also a cavalier attitude by the railway companies. In their lack of concern with regard to how the work got done as long as it *did* get done, they were as culpable as the man at the rock face.

When and Where
About 9.30 on the evening of Saturday 14 October 1876. In the north of Bottesford heading of No.2 Shaft of Hose Tunnel near Scalford, in the county of Leicester, on a joint line of the Great Northern and London and North Western Railway companies, intended to run from Melton Mowbray to Bottesford.

Who – The Men

Eight men were working: John Foster, 'Scandulous' Samuel/
William Longman and John Sismey were at work at the upper
lift; Samuel Lee, Charles Finch and Robert Cann were about
3 or 4 yards from the face of the lower lift, and therefore about
6 to 8 yards behind the first three, these were engaged in
timbering up or supporting the sides and roof with planks;
William Taylor was some 3 yards further back running out
earth; and Thomas Wheeler, the foreman of the shift, was
about 15 yards behind.[6]

How – Setting the Scene

Blasting usually took place twice during each shift. It was the
practice to take the gunpowder into the tunnel, when the
holes were ready to be charged, in a can holding 12–14lbs.

The can had a long projecting neck with a sliding cover,
which would hold about 8 or 10oz of gunpowder, and was
called a 'tot' by the workmen. It served as a measure of the
amount of gunpowder to be used, three or four tots being
sufficient for a charge. After being poured from the can into
the tots, the gunpowder was projected out with force by
striking the tots against the side of the hole. The object of this
was to ensure the gunpowder reached the bottom of the hole
and to prevent it from adhering to the sides.

On the upper lift, where the explosion occurred, Sismey,
having made a hole obliquely in the earth on the bottom
(which would explode upwards), had already charged it with
gunpowder and was stemming it with clay, sitting down for
the purpose behind Longman, who was in the act of charging
another hole in the face of the tunnel.[7]

Why – Three Candles and a Lot of Gunpowder

Near to Sismey there were two candles a short distance apart
on the ground, and Longman was lighted by a candle placed in
the rock face about 2ft from his hole and a little above it. Foster

was working at the side. The can containing the gunpowder (around 12–14lbs) was on the ground close by.

Longman, having filled the tot for the third or fourth time, attempted to project the contents into the hole. In so doing he accidentally struck it against some projecting earth on the face of the tunnel and scattered the gunpowder around, which, coming into contact with either his or one of Sismey's candles, was ignited, causing the explosion.

The gunpowder still remaining in the can also exploded, as did that in Longman's hole and presumably that in Sismey's hole on the ground.

Health and Safety?
Thomas Wheeler, ganger, told the coroner's court: 'It was my habit to *tell all the men to be careful* every time they charged the holes. It was no part of my duty to see where the candles were placed in the tunnel.'[8]

Major A. Ford, RA, HM's Inspector of Explosives Report
Where a tunnel takes several months to construct, and the details of the working in the shafts are left to the foreman of each gang, and no rules or regulations are issued by the contractors, there cannot be much doubt that considerable supervision is necessary.

As regards Longman, it cannot be said that he exercised due prudence and caution when charging his hole by 'projecting' the gunpowder into it under the circumstances stated. But it must be admitted that the method he adopted was the recognised plan in the tunnel; he had become accustomed to charge his holes with the candle at no greater distance, and never thought it possible that he should scatter the gunpowder by striking the face of the tunnel. A stranger to this method of working would no doubt have thought differently, and have rightly considered it a most dangerous practice; but Longman had become used to it, and considered it safe, and immunity from accidents hitherto had so far favoured this view … On the whole, therefore, although there is no doubt that great blame attaches to Longman for his want of caution, it is, in my opinion, scarcely such as would render him criminally responsible. The primary responsibility in the matter appears to me to attach to Messrs Benton and Woodiwiss.[9]

Outcome

The three men on the upper lift were all very seriously injured, two fatally; Foster died on 28 October 1876 and Sismey on 3 November; Longman, who received the discharge of the gunpowder in his face, was hospitalised in a dangerous condition, but on 13 December he had recovered sufficiently to be able to give an account of the accident at the inquest; the three men on the lower lift, Lee, Finch and Cann, were so badly injured that they had not returned to work more than a month after the incident; the foreman, who was upwards of 20 yards from the can when the gunpowder exploded, was also burnt.

Verdict

The coroner's jury found that the deceased, John Foster, died from the effects of burns caused by an explosion of blasting powder in Hose Tunnel, and that such explosion was caused by the carelessness of Samuel Longman, but that such carelessness does not amount to criminality. They further add that in their opinion 'based upon the evidence brought before them', the mode of performing blasting operations in the said tunnel is defective in arrangement, and during its progress lacks proper supervision. They recommend that cartridges be used in lieu of loose blasting powder. But in the event of such powder continuing to be used in a loose state, that not more than 4lbs be sent into the tunnel at one time to one set or gang of men, and that properly protected lamps be used instead of naked candles.

The jury request Her Majesty's inspector who has attended this inquest to forward this expression of their opinion to the Secretary of State for the Home Department, and that the coroner forward it to the tunnel contractors.

Conclusion
Major A. Ford, RA, HM's Inspector of Explosives

> Had there been no more than four pounds of gunpowder in
> the can taken into the tunnel at the time when the accident
> to which this report relates occurred, as would have been
> the case had it been a mine within the meaning of those
> Acts (Mines Regulations Acts (35 & 36 Vict. cc. 76 and
> 77) I have little doubt that both the men whose lives were
> sacrificed would have escaped, and probably nearly all of
> the other six men would have been uninjured.

Dynamite

Dynamite started life as nitroglycerine. This interesting compound was created accidentally by Italian chemist Ascanio Sobrero in 1847 when he worked glycerol with a mixture of nitric and sulphuric acid. The combination produced an oily, colourless explosive liquid, which was highly volatile and so unstable that the smallest jolt, friction or impact could cause it to explode.

Alfred Nobel, a Swedish chemical engineer, met Sobrero in Paris some three years after this discovery and was intrigued by its possibilities. The breakthrough came when Nobel found that by using kieselguhr (a type of soft rock containing the remains of particular diatoms with cell walls of silica), which absorbed the nitroglycerine, he had a malleable, more predictable material that could be formed into suitable shapes for different commercial uses.

Alfred Nobel called this substance 'dynamite' and patented it in 1867. To discharge the dynamite he invented a blasting cap, or detonator, which could be ignited by lighting a fuse. Nobel believed that his new dynamite would bring real benefits as not only would it cut the costs of many forms of construction work that required blasting, but it would also reduce the number of injuries and deaths resulting from the blasting process.[10]

By the later decades of the nineteenth century, tunnel-making dynamite was proving to be more popular than gunpowder and guncotton – although all of these were sometimes used in the same tunnel. The *Western Daily Express* reported: 'The dynamite "blew" to the very bottom of the hole, and thus made a gain of some inches in every set of charges. The dynamite also cuts away the blasted rock cleaner, from the roof and from the sides, thus leaving few powder shakes and loose pieces behind.'[11]

Despite Nobel's hopes, dynamite was viewed as (and proved to be) an especially dangerous substance, and, as with gunpowder, one had to have a licence to procure, hold and use it. The licence came with numbered conditions. The Home Office Explosives Department had been set up in 1871. It was led by their explosives expert, Colonel Sir Vivian Dering Majendie, something of a hero.[12] Col Majendie, a retired military man previously of the Royal Artillery, had already written several books on explosive materials and armaments before he took up the post. He was also influential in framing the updated Explosives Act of 1875.

Cymmer Tunnel – Fifteen Persons Killed

Hampshire Telegraph and Sussex Chronicle, **26 April 1876**
A serious accident with dynamite occurred on Friday night [21 April 1876] between eight and nine o'clock at the Tunnel works of the Bridgend and Ogmore Railway at Blaewn Llanvi, South Wales. The tunnel is being driven by

the Diamond Rock Drill Company ... about thirty hands were working at the time, one half of whom never more saw light of day, and the remainder who were the men in the advanced heading, came out through the poisonous fumes of the after gases of explosions, in a very exhausted and almost fainting condition.[13]

The accident was of a most horrendous and deadly nature.

There were nine gangs each of nearly forty men who were employed over three shifts at that period. The night shift had just gone into the workings and it was those who were working in the bottom heading that were killed. The explosion was enormous, blowing the timber framing literally out of the tunnel, and a whole truck of stone was smashed and driven a good way back. The blast was heard miles around. Initially it was unclear whether the explosion was a result of a man lighting his pipe and dropping the match, or dropping his lighted candle onto the powder. The damage done to the tunnel was extensive, but, more seriously, the number of dead was high – thirteen people died horribly and others were dreadfully injured. A search party went in to look for them, or what they could find of them, under all the blown apart debris. It was not easy, and a very unpleasant task. Of the young boy, Clement, who was bringing in some tools at the time, very little was found.

With so many dead, and with dynamite involved, it required an extensive investigation by HM Inspector of Explosives. Colonel Majendie turned the accident into a possible crime scene, as his raison d'être was to see if a crime had been committed and, if so, by whom, and then to bring them to justice.[14] He was the equivalent of today's CSI, and his investigations, like those of all railway inspectors (such as Major A. Ford's at Hose) were thorough, his reports detailed and often critical (again like the later Major Ford's).

REPORT
by V.D. Majendie, Major RA, HM's Inspector of Explosives

I have held an inquiry into the circumstances attending an explosion of dynamite which occurred at Cymmer, near Maesteg, Glamorganshire, on the 21st April 1876, by which 13 persons lost their lives and two others were injured.

I beg to furnish the following report –

Circumstances under which the explosion occurred –

The explosion took place in an unfinished tunnel, forming part of the Llynvi and Ogmore Railway Extension. This tunnel which, when completed, will be nearly a mile in length, is being driven through a high hill lying between Maesteg and Cymmer by the Diamond Rock Boring Company (Limited), of 2 Westminster Chambers, Victoria Street, SW. The work at the time of the accident was being carried on from both ends, and at the north or Cymmer end a distance of 365 yards had been penetrated. At 8.30pm on the 21st April an explosion occurred at a manhole, situated in, and on the left side of, the tunnel, 176 yards from the mouth, by which 13 persons were instantaneously killed and two others sustained serious injuries. Some damage also was done to the tunnel, portions of the roof of the heading being injured, in one case at a distance of 118 yards from the scene of the explosion, and the wooden centres at the opening of the tunnel distant 176 yards being blown away.

The names of the persons who were killed were:

John Bartle	30 years	body or remains found 18 feet from scene of explosion
Robert Quick	25 years	body or remains found about 81 feet from scene of explosion
Joseph Pearce	25 years	body or remains found about 81 feet from scene of explosion
Robert Weeks	30 years	body or remains found about 111 feet from scene of explosion

Edward Morgan 32 years body or remains found about 81 feet from scene of explosion

Evan Davies 41 years body or remains found about 111 feet from scene of explosion

John Osborne 25 years body or remains found about 81 feet from scene of explosion

George Moore 20 years body or remains found about 81 feet from scene of explosion

David Hitchins unknown body or remains found about 111 feet from scene of explosion

Morgan Jones 19 years body or remains found about 111 feet from scene of explosion

Richard Parsons 29 years body or remains found opposite scene of explosion

James Oates unknown body or remains found about 81 feet from scene of explosion

John Clements 13 years body or remains found opposite scene of explosion

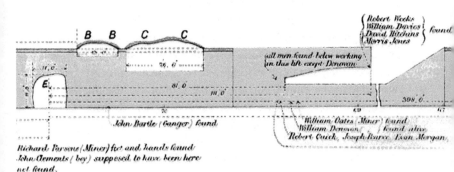

After the accident had occurred, William Elliott, the foreman at the Cymmer end of the tunnel, and others, were prompt in removing the injured men, and Elliott especially seems to have displayed great presence of mind and gallantry. Immediately on the accident occurring he

gave instructions to the engineman to keep up a strong blast of fresh air into the tunnel; and he himself worked at the removal of the bodies and of the injured men until he was overpowered and rendered insensible by the noxious gases which the explosion of the dynamite had produced.

Arrangements of the Company for the storage and supply of explosives –

[…] it appears that the work which was being carried on by the Company involved the use of a considerable quantity of explosive. Both *gunpowder* and *dynamite* were employed for the purpose; and at the time of the accident the Company also had some *Cotton powder* in their possession. Two magazines existed for the storage of the explosives, both being at the Maesteg side of the tunnel and distant over a mile from the Cymmer end. One of these magazines is used for the storage of dynamite; the other is used for the storage of gunpowder and cotton powder. The two magazines form separate buildings, more than 100 yards apart. The dynamite magazine existed in virtue of a special license No. 322, granted under the Nitro-Glycerine Act, 1869 (32 & 33 Vict. c. 113), and dated 25th August 1875. This license being limited in duration to 12 months …

The gunpowder magazine does not appear to have been covered by any license under the old Act, or by any license or registration under the new Act, and the storing of cotton powder (exceeding the amount which may be kept for private use and not for sale) without license or registration, was also illegal.

The practice appears to have been for the foremen respectively in charge of the two ends of the tunnel to draw supplies of explosive for their use from the magazine. At the Maesteg end of the tunnel, the foreman generally drew only a small quantity of explosive, about enough for 12 hours working, and this was deposited in a wooden box a little way within the tunnel, a packet being brought from the box to a little wooden shed outside, for the purpose of fitting the detonators and fuse for firing. I am not strictly concerned with this end of the tunnel, except in so far as the practice there bears upon the practice at the other end; but I cannot refrain from noticing the almost entire absence of precautions which I observed there. The box where the packages of dynamite are placed for use, contained, at the time of my visit, candles, fuse, old iron and rubbish and dirt of various descriptions; while the wooden shed, in which the charges were made up was a sort of general store, full of iron, spades, pickaxes, and other implements. There was also a stove in it, but this I was assured is never used. It is clear, however, that at the Maesteg end of the tunnel, the precautions for preventing accidents by explosion were at a minimum; and no attempt seems to have been made by the issue of suitable instructions to enforce care and caution.

Turning to the Cymmer end of the tunnel, it appears that the manhole where the explosion occurred had been specially appropriated to the reception of the dynamite as it was received from the magazine at the Maesteg end; and it was fitted with a door and lock. The detonators and fuse were also kept here, the former being placed on a small shelf made for the purpose in the upper part of the manhole. Elliott, the foreman at this end, states that it was an instruction to the men to prepare their charges not at the manhole where the dynamite was kept, but at another manhole 40 feet further in the tunnel. This instruction, it was stated has emanated from Mr Lean the engineer.

The powder which was drawn from the magazine appears to have been kept in a separate place, some of it being in a manhole 80 feet nearer the entrance of the tunnel than the dynamite manhole.

***The next question is, what quantity of explosive was kept
in the manhole; and what were the precautions enjoined or
observed with regard to it.***

The former of these points is of importance, not merely as
bearing upon the loss of life and extent of damage produced
by this explosion, but as affecting the question of the legality
of the presence of a quantity of dynamite within the tunnel.
The other point is of importance in regard to the light
which it may throw upon the cause of the accident, and in
its relation to the question of whether *blame attaches to the
Company or their responsible officers or servants for this explosion.*

[...] there is, I think, no doubt that the quantity of
dynamite actually present in the manhole at the time of the
explosion was 150lbs. An issue of 200lbs of dynamite had
been made from the magazine by Butland, the storekeeper,
on the 18th April; and of this quantity, Elliott states 50lbs
and no more had been used up to the time of the accident.
There were also in the manhole about 10lbs of cotton
powder, some detonators and fuse. The whole of these were
exploded or destroyed by the explosion.

It is clear, therefore, from the above that there had been
placed in the manhole on the 18th a quantity of dynamite
sufficient for several days consumption; because while
the quantity so deposited was 200lbs, it appears that the
actual consumption from the 18th to the 21st (3 days) only
equalled 50lbs. This fact it will be my duty to comment
upon more closely hereafter.

Majendie then states that although the manhole had a locked
door and the key was held by the foremen, Elliott and Bartle,
they had a habit of giving the key to other workmen who
would go and get whatever dynamite they wanted, often by
the light of a naked candle. In fact the foremen gave them no
'instructions of care'.

He found it unbelievable that the unsuitable, unlined
manhole (put in for the safety of railwaymen when the

trains were running) was used not just as 'a place of deposit' for the explosives, but also as a space for preparation of the charges, i.e. by the fitting together of the detonators, fuse and dynamite. Not only that, they did this preparation work by the light of a naked flame - a candle stuck against the wall just outside the entrance – and whilst smoking. Richard Parson was guilty on both accounts, many times, but only received a verbal reprimand from the foremen.

As to the precautions taken to prevent accidents, he said they were 'very much less stringent than is necessary to afford even a reasonable measure of security against accidents'.

Cause of explosion –

With regard to the cause of this explosion, there is evidence that Parsons at the time it occurred was again doing, in defiance of orders, he was engaged in preparing his primers at the manhole in which the supply of dynamite was deposited. William Lewis, a collier by trade, happened to have gone into the tunnel a few minutes before the explosion. As he passed the manhole he observed Parsons sitting on the sill of the manhole, and he had some conversation with him. Parsons was engaged in making up his charges, he had the detonators and fuse to his left hand, and immediately above the little accumulation of explosives, and about 6in from the side of the manhole, he had his naked candle stuck against the wall in the usual way by a piece of clay. It is significant of the general disregard of precautions which prevailed, that Lewis should have selected a man engaged on this work as the person from whom he could most conveniently obtain a light for his candle; and it is significant also of Parsons' general recklessness, that he should not only have been ready to give him a light, but that while so engaged, he should have invited his particular attention to the detonators and other explosive material lying beside him … after which, in a few minutes the explosion occurred. The fact that the remains of Parsons, blown almost to pieces, were found close to the manhole, tends to show that he was, at the time of the explosion, still engaged upon the work which had occupied him when Lewis passed. Such being the case, it really seems unnecessary to have recourse to recondite suggestions to explain the cause of this terrible explosion. I am not aware that it has ever been seriously suggested that the explosion was the result of spontaneous ignition; but, as this theory is rather a favourite one on such occasions, I thought it desirable to submit to Dr Dupre a sample of the dynamite from the same batch as that which exploded (taken from the magazine at the Maesteg end) for chemical examination. That gentleman's report shows that the dynamite was of satisfactory quality, and free from any indications of destructive chemical action, or of the presence of any elements which would justify suspicion in this direction.

We are then left with our choice of the following possible explanations –
1: That, through some carelessness or clumsiness, Parsons exploded a detonator as he was fitting a fuse into it, or as he was fixing it in a primer
2: That a spark was communicated in some way to one or other of the explosives present
3: That the explosion was produced by a blow
4: That the candle fell onto and fired one or other of the explosives, thereby causing the explosion of the whole.

As regards the *first possible cause*, it is not impossible that the explosion may have proceeded from it, but it is certainly the most improbable of the four possible explanations enumerated above.

As regards the *second possible cause*, I ascertained by experiment not only that a spark can readily be struck with a piece of steel against the 'Pennant' stone (a hard sandstone), in which the manhole was excavated, but that even two pieces of the stone itself struck smartly together are liable to give a spark.

Or, *thirdly*, the same drill would have been capable of exploding the dynamite by a blow.

Dr Dupre's report shows that dynamite of this quality can be exploded by a 1lb steel weight falling on to it a height of 18 inches. Or, the drill falling into the detonators might have produced an explosion.

It is, of course, impossible to say that it was not so caused, but I venture to think that the falling of a candle (either that belonging to Parsons, or that carried by the boy) on to the little pile of detonators, fuse, and dynamite, is by far the most probable of the four suggested causes.

Persons who have not actually made the experiment can hardly be aware of the silent rapidity with which the burning of a portion of ignited dynamite proceeds. And this observation holds good also with regard to gun-cotton. I am satisfied from my experiments that had a primer of dynamite (or gun-cotton) fitted with a detonator become ignited, it would scarcely have been possible for any person who might be close by to have effected their escape before the explosion which would be the necessary consequence of such ignition took place. I may add that I have also ascertained by actual experiment that a lighted candle falling on to dynamite almost instantly ignites it.

Considering, therefore, that it is established that there existed all the elements for the production of an explosion in this way – the naked candle stuck against the wall by means of clay (to say nothing of the candle probably in the boy's hand), the dynamite and the detonators, and almost certainly some primers already fitted with detonators, it seems unnecessary to have recourse to such explanations as the falling of a steel drill, or the accidental explosion of detonators to account for the explosion.

There can be very little reasonable doubt that the explosion was produced by the falling of a candle (or a spark therefrom) on to some of the explosive present, probably on to a primer of dynamite with detonator fixed, and that the resulting explosion extended to the whole of the explosives within the manhole.

That the large quantity of dynamite present increased the loss of life, I have no doubt. It will be observed that the large proportion of the men who were killed were working at a distance of from 80 to 111 feet from the scene of the explosion, and it is further noticeable that of the men working at this distance two escaped with their lives. *I am accordingly led to the conclusion that had the quantity of dynamite present been very much less than that which actually exploded, the lives of the whole of the 10 men who were working at these distances from the scene of the explosion would most probably have been saved.*

What blame attaches to the Company or their servants for this sad explosion and loss of life?

The Coroner's Jury, after about an hour's deliberation, returned the following verdict:

'That the deceased died from suffocation and shock, the result of an explosion of dynamite, but how caused there is not sufficient evidence to show.' I feel constrained to say that this verdict falls very far short of the meeting the justice of the case; and I must profess my surprise that the jury did not consider that the evidence which was laid before them at the inquest called for a more decided verdict, or at least made imperative some strong expression of opinion as to the general manner in which that part of the business of the Company which was connected with the storage and management of explosives was shown to have been carried on.

I conceive it to be my duty to point out that the Company appear not only to have been guilty of certain violations of the law, one of which I cannot doubt contributed to augment the loss of life resulting from this accident; but that they are also chargeable with an amount of carelessness and negligence in the management of the explosives kept and used by them which calls for a strong expression of censure and fixes on them a most serious responsibility in connection with this accident.

As regards the illegalities which I conceive were committed, it appears –

1st. That the Company at the time of the accident were storing gunpowder and cotton powder without any license or authority. I have stated that they possessed a gunpowder magazine, and it appears from a return furnished to me by the Company of the issues of explosive to the Cymmer end of the tunnel, that the consumption of powder was considerable. It appears therefrom that there were constant issues of 2cwt of gunpowder at a time. Thus, in January, there were six such issues, making 12cwt; in February there were four such issues, making 8cwt; in March there was one issue of 2cwt; and in April (up to the 21st) there were three such issues, or 6cwt. Thus the total issues of gunpowder from 1st January to 21st April amounted to 28cwt. Under the Explosives Act, which came into operation on the 1st January last, no person may keep more than 30lbs of gunpowder without a license or under registration, and then only provided it is kept for private use and not for sale. It is clear, therefore, that (not to go further back than the 1st January) the Company had been illegally storing gunpowder. They had also, it appears, been illegally storing gun-cotton (or 'cotton powder'), for on the 17th April there was an issue to the Cymmer end of 56lbs of 'patent gun-cotton' and '100 cartridges compressed ditto'. Of this material the Explosives Act allows only 15lbs to be kept (for private use and not for sale) without license or registration (Order in Council No.8).

With regard to this, however, Mr Lean laid some stress on the fact that the Company had, prior to 31st March, made application for a store license to cover the storage of 'Mixed Explosives', which license they have failed to obtain owing to the proposed site not being strictly in accordance with the provisions of the Order in Council relating to Stores. But it is proper to point out that the keeping of this gunpowder without a license had not only constituted an illegality since 1st January 1876, but was illegal under the old Act which expired at that date (see 23 & 24 Vict. c. 139, sec. XVIII.), and the mere fact of applying for a license about the end of March would not excuse the previous illegality, nor cover the continued storage of the explosive preceding the grant of such license, or after it had failed to be obtained.

2nd. [...] a more serious illegality, in my judgment, consisted in the storing of quantities of dynamite in the manhole at the Cymmer end of the tunnel. A reference to the license held by the Company shows that Condition 3 directs that Nitro-glycerine preparations stored in pursuance of this license shall – 'not be stored anywhere than in a certain magazine well and substantially built of brick or stone, or excavated in solid rock, earth, or mine refuse, and lined throughout with wood, and situated at Blaen Llynvi, near Maesteg, in the parish of Llangonoyd, in the county of Glamorgan' and Condition 11 directs as follows – 'Nitro-glycerine preparations stored under this license shall not be used except by the licensee or persons in his immediate employ; and shall not be sold or served out except to persons in the immediate employ of the licensee for the immediate use of such persons on work authorised by the licensee.'

This brings me to the question – What is immediate use? The resident engineer Mr Lean, who naturally in the interests of the Company would be disposed to assign a liberal interpretation to this expression, appeared to consider that 'immediate use' meant about a day's (24 hours) consumption.

Elliott stated that he had received verbal instructions from Mr Lean not to get more than two boxes (=100lbs in all) at one time. This, at the rate of consumption which had obtained up to the date of the accident, would generally represent four or more days consumption. Mr Lean, however, states that he does not recollect giving Elliott these instructions, and thinks it improbable that he would have given an order for any definite limit of quantity without regard to the actual consumption … it is quite clear that, as a matter of fact, no correspondence between the quantity required for 'immediate use' and the quantity actually issued was observed on the occasion of the last issue or on former occasions.

An analysis of the return gives the following results –
January – Total issues between 3rd January and 3rd February, 650lbs. If we assume that the consumption proceeded at the same rate, we have for the 31 days an average consumption of about 21lbs a day. But in no case were the issues less than 50lbs, or two days consumption, and in one case (the 14th), 100lbs was issued.

There were in the month, 11 issues of 50lbs, = over 2 days each, and 1 issue of 100lbs, = nearly five days.

February – Total issues and (assumed) consumption from 3rd February to 1st March, 750lbs, = average consumption for the 26 days, 29lbs per diem. But the actual issues were –
7 of 50lbs = over 1½ days each
2 of 100lbs = about 3½ days each
1 of 200lbs = about 7 days

March – From 1st March to 4th April, issues and (assumed) consumption, 550lbs, making an average consumption for the 34 days of 16lbs a day. But the whole of this amount was served out in only five issues, being –
1 of 30lbs = about 1½ days
4 of 100lbs = about 6½ days each

April – Issues from 4th to 21st, 550lbs.

Of this 150lbs was destroyed by the explosion, leaving 400lbs expended between the 4th and 21st, and giving an average consumption for the 17 days of 22lbs a day.

The issues during this month were –

1 of 50lbs = 2 days consumption

3 of 100lbs = 4 days consumption

1 of 200lbs = 8 days consumption

I do not lose sight of the fact that this mode of exhibiting the want of correspondence between the issues and the quantities required for 'immediate use' is open to the objection that being based upon the 'average' rate of consumption it takes no account of the occasionally heavy expenditures of dynamite, or of the days when there was no such expenditure at all.

It may be represented, for example, that although 100lbs was issued on the 14th January when the average consumption was only 21lbs a day, there is nothing to show that the whole of that 100lbs was not, in fact, used on the 14th or 15th. But this argument, if it be admitted, includes also the admission that the consumption was exceedingly variable, and subject to no very reliable rule of averages, and it follows, therefore, that the storekeeper, in the absence of definite information as to the actual consumption or immediate requirements, could not possibly have adjusted his issues to the real requirements for 'immediate use'. In the absence of any such information he would have nothing whatever to go upon but his calculation as to the rate at which the dynamite was demanded, and at which, judging from the frequency or infrequency of these demands, its use was proceeding; and the above tables at any rate show that if he in fact proceeded upon this method of calculation he certainly made no attempt to observe any relation between his issues and the amount apparently required for immediate use, seeing that he actually made his issues in quantities varying from one and a half to eight days average consumption. Had the storekeeper then anything else to guide him? It appears that he had not. It was the practice of the foreman, Elliott, when he wanted dynamite, to make a requisition on a form provided in a book; but it was not his practice to specify the amount required, nor had the storekeeper, whose magazine was distant about a mile (over rough mountain road) from the Cymmer end, any other opportunity of ascertaining with any sort of accuracy what was being actually used. And as a matter of fact it appeared from my examination of the storekeeper that he was even ignorant of the particular condition of the license which required the issues to be thus regulated.

Still, despite the probability, almost certainty, that this condition must under the circumstances have failed to be observed, and despite its apparent non-observance throughout the three and a half months preceding the explosion, as ascertained by the method of computation adopted above, I deemed necessary to examine a little closer and to inform myself whether there actually was, on the particular occasion in question, a non-observance of this rule. The storekeeper's book shows that there was an issue to the Cymmer end, on the 18th April, of 200lbs of dynamite.

— Elliott stated that on receiving this large amount he was at a loss what to do with it, and would have sent some of it back, but he considered he had no authority to do so.

— There had been nothing in Elliott's requisition to suggest the sending of this large quantity.

— It is true there had been a slight delay in the obtaining of dynamite from the agent at Cardiff.

—There was also the fact that the chairman of the Company (Major Beaumont) was known to the storekeeper to be present and carrying out experiments with new drills, and there was thus on his mind an impression that the stock had run out, and that the occasion was one when probably an extra supply would be useful.

As a matter of fact both these surmises were incorrect, for there still remained (Elliott says) 50lbs of dynamite when the new supply was received, and there was in fact no increase whatever in the actual rate of consumption for that month.

These circumstances alone, show how impossible it was for a storekeeper, without definite instructions and a proper system, to have observed this important condition. Moreover, the license leaves no room for guesses and conjectures of this sort. It expressly prohibits the issue of larger quantities than are required for immediate use; not quantities larger than the storekeeper or other person may consider or conjecture to be necessary, but quantities not exceeding what actually is necessary.

Negligence of the company and their servants with regards to the management of explosives

Majendie took his position and responsibilities very seriously and considered it his 'duty' to make it clear where there was 'negligence' or 'laxity' – he found there was both to a considerable degree at Cymmer. He also found that:

— the foreman who was charged with the receipt and custody of the dynamite had neither received nor issued any written instructions with regard to its management;
— a suggestion which Elliott says he had made to Mr Lean that a small supplementary magazine should be provided outside the tunnel was not adopted; – the manhole beyond being provided with a door and lock was not fitted in any way as even a place of temporary deposit for explosive should be, whether the explosive so deposited be in large or small quantities;
— the detonators were kept inside the manhole with the dynamite;
— the whole business of the place was permitted to be carried on by the light of naked candles;

— smoking, which in theory was prohibited, could, as it appears, be indulged in in the manhole with impunity;
— while even repeated disregard of the orders which had been given against preparing the charges at this manhole entailed upon the offenders no more serious consequences than a verbal reprimand.

Majendie found the company guilty of considerable neglect and 'habitual carelessness' towards both their responsibility with regard to the care of the explosives and their responsibility with regard to the safety of their workmen. He dismissed the company's pleas of 'ignorance of the sort of precautions which should have been observed' and stated that by their casual behaviour they had 'laid themselves open to very grave censure'.

He had no patience with the arguments and suggestions of Mr Lean, the resident engineer, regarding the better light given by a candle as against a lamp, finding that they 'rested upon no substantial basis', pointing out that:

Had he taken any trouble on the subject, he would have discovered that two patterns of lamps had been approved by me on behalf of the Secretary of State, and that the illuminating power of either of them was vastly superior to that of the common tallow candles actually employed. He would also have found that these lamps might be brought into even close proximity to an explosive without danger. In fact, he would have found that his argument on this point was worthless.

He takes them all to task over the dangerous practice of storing the dynamite in the tunnel rather than outside and finally concludes:

When all has been said, the conclusion appears inevitable that serious blame attaches to the Company and their servants for the dangerous negligence which is shown to have prevailed at these works in regard to the keeping and handling of explosives.

It was surely the duty of the Company to satisfy themselves that adequate precautions have been adopted for the prevention of accidents. Had the Company made any inquiry of this sort, I cannot doubt that they must have seen reason, as they can hardly fail to see reason now, for dissatisfaction with the arrangements. The professional qualifications of the chairman (Major Beaumont, RE) and his experience in connection with explosives, would at once have suggested to him that the arrangements adopted were not such as to afford any reasonable security against a serious accident.

The actual working arrangements were, however, in the hands of Mr Lean, the resident engineer, and it does appear to me that this gentleman is seriously to blame for the state of things which prevailed. It was, in my opinion, his duty to have taken steps to secure the strict observance of the conditions of the license and the adoption of proper measures of precaution..

There was thus, as it appears to me, a general failure of duty and censurable negligence on the part of all concerned, beginning with the Company, continuing with Mr Lean, Butland (the storekeeper), and Elliott, and ending with Parsons, and to the failure of duty and negligence of this last-named man in the careless and improper making up of the charges at the manhole, the explosion, as I have shown, may be immediately ascribed, while the large resulting loss of life was no doubt due to the direct violation of a condition of the license and the illegal presence of a quantity of dynamite largely in excess of what was required for 'immediate use'.[15]

FIRE

Welwyn Tunnel – 'A Calamity So Astounding'

The Times was generally not known for dramatic or excessive theatrical reportage, even during the highly graphic nineteenth-century reportage period, but it felt obliged to described this accident on the night of Saturday 9 June 1866 as 'a calamity so astounding as to be almost incredible were it not that it is undeniably true'. *The Times* was not alone in its astonishment. The accident caused enormous excitement, curiosity and a great deal of concern among the local population; this is unsurprising as it was reported as 'an accident of the most alarming and unprecedented kind' ,[1] whilst the *Illustrated London News* called it 'an accident of a strangely complicated nature'. The general manager of the Great Northern Railway (on whose line the tunnel lay), a Mr Seymour Clarke, on the other hand, when reporting on the incident in a letter to that paper, described the 'calamity' with clever, managerial British understatement; he explained it as merely 'a serious obstruction'.

The Railway Inspectorate's Lt Col F.H. Rich, who made the 'rigid enquiry' Mr Clarke referred to, summed up 'the calamity' in the usual format as follows:

Accident Returns: Extract for Accident at Welwyn Tunnel on 9 June 1866

This document was published on 30 June 1866 by the Board of Trade. It was written by Lt Col F.H. Rich.

Location: Welwyn Tunnel
Train Operator: Great Northern Railway
Primary Cause: Train breakdown
Secondary Cause: Inadequate signalling arrangements
Result: Rear collision, derailment, head on collision, fire
            2 fatalities, 2 injured

Welwyn Tunnel (which is actually two lengthy tunnels, Southern Tunnel and Northern Tunnel, within 300 yards of each other) lies some five miles beyond Hatfield (and just twenty or so miles from London) between Welwyn Junction and Stevenage on the Great Northern Railway line. At the entrance of the down line was a signal box. At this time in 1866 traffic the tunnel was operated using block working. It should have been impossible for three trains to be together in the same tunnel at the same time. The Great Northern Railway Company had a better-than-most reputation in the railway world. Luckily this incredible calamity was confined to three goods trains, had it been otherwise, the loss of life would have been horrendous.

The *first* train involved in the accident consisted of empty coal wagons, drawn by a tender locomotive. On Saturday night travelling on the down-line, around 11.20 p.m. it was signalled through from Welwyn and entered the second, long Northern tunnel. About midway in it came to an enforced stop, owing to engine failure – a boiler-tube on the engine had burst. The guard, Joseph Wray/Ray, suggested that the train be allowed to roll back on the falling gradient to Welwyn, but the driver refused, knowing it could cost him his job.

The *second* train was a Midland Railway goods train from London, with wagons carrying a variety of things, including highly inflammable materials. At 11.36 p.m., it stopped at Welwyn signal box. By some mistake or neglect the signalman at Welwyn, allowed the second train into the tunnel. (He told the inquest that he had sent a telegraph message to Knebworth asking if the coal train had cleared the tunnel. He said that he believed he had been told 'train out', he therefore lowered his signals.) The goods train hit the rear end of the coal truck at around 20–25 mph; the force of the impact caused a number of its own wagons to be thrown over and block the up line, whilst spilling open its contents, including casks of oil.

The *third* train was a Great Northern express freight train, with a large number of trucks, carrying meat from Scotland for Smithfield Market in London. As no one knew of the already catastrophe existing in the tunnel, it entered without hesitation and at speed, and smashed into the debris of the Midland train. Its engine was overturned, and the coal and cinders from its furnace flew out and were scattered over all.

Altogether eighty-six wagons/trucks on all three trains, made mostly of wood, were involved. These combined with hot-lighted coals, casks of oil, and numerous carcasses of meat, were all converted into 'a huge enormous bonfire',[2] and, being just beneath one of the tunnel's ventilation shafts, the drafts of air fanned the flames so that at times they could be seen up the shaft leaping into the night air.

Amazingly the drivers and firemen of all three engines had escaped either unhurt or with only slight injuries. It was also surprising, due to the nature of the trains, that there were very relatively few casualties:

The guard Wray, who was found in the midst ruins of his break, frightfully crushed and dead, and with him another man, a fireman in the employ of the Metropolitan Railway, whom it appears he was conveying surreptitiously down the line to his home, who, although not quite dead, was in a dying condition and was not expected to survive many hours. The guard of the Northern up train, Lacey, was also found lying, on the line near the track, most severely injured about the head.[3]

The drivers and the firemen had got the information back to the signal boxes and the news was sent out to all the necessary officials of the companies. Mr Johnson, the chief engineer, came from Barnet, and Mr Seymour Clarke, general manager, from Hatfield, both arrived in the early hours of the morning to assess the situation.

The situation that confronted them was an appalling one. From the mouth of the tunnel suffocating clouds of smoke and waves of intense heat were issuing. And the sound which came from within was like the roar of a mighty cataract. At intervals, too, came the terrifying reports of explosions. Finding it impossible to effect an entrance at this end, Messrs Clarke and Johnson led their men over the fields to where the rails again issued near Knebworth, and as they scaled the high ground beneath which the tunnel passes they saw flames every now and then emerge from the top of the air-shaft. This, they knew, was more than eighty feet above the level of the rails.[4]

At the Knebworth end they and the gang of some 200 men they had collected, were able to get inside and pull out some of the still upright meat wagons before being forced back by the heat. The fire raged with 'terrible violence' all day. One of the unfortunate things was that there was only one fire engine available and that was some distance. It was a small one belonging to the Marquis of Salisbury's Hatfield estate, and it took some time to be brought, and there was no water source to feed it. It was decided to let the fire burn itself out. Not until evening did they set to work at the south end, when water was brought by engines in tenderfulls.

It was not until 6 p.m. on Sunday, seventeen hours after the collisions, that an entry could be effected from the south end of the tunnel. Then Mr Johnson and Mr Budge of the locomotive department led in a gang of about 450 navvies and mechanics, and soon a sufficient amount of the outlying debris was cleared away to allow the fire engine to be brought to bear upon the centre of the fire – a smouldering and still sometimes flaming mass beneath the airshaft. When this was at last deadened, two powerful cranes were brought in to assist in the removal of the heavier wreckage.[5]

All this drama was watched by large crowds of people. The drama continued as the Great Northern struggled to re-route all the trains, having to call in lots of favours to do so. Luckily the Sunday traffic was usually light, but it would be 'business as usual' albeit by a circuitous, much longer route, the Company was anxious to reassure the public.

From the General Manager of the Great Northern Railway

TO THE EDITOR OF *THE TIMES*

Sir, – A serious obstruction occurred on the Great Northern Railway on Saturday night, in the Welwyn tunnel, about 20 miles from London, under the following circumstances:-

A train of empty coal waggons was going northwards through the tunnel, when the engine burst a tube and was unable to proceed. A goods train was following, and, by some mistake on the part of the signalman (at present un-explained), was allowed to enter the tunnel before the signalman had received the telegraphic message from the other end of it that the preceding train had passed out. The train came into collision with the brake-van of the empty waggons, throwing the van and several waggons of the first train and the engine of the second train off the line.

The guard of the first train was killed. At this moment a goods train reached the north end of the tunnel, and, there was nothing to indicate an obstruction of the 'up line it was allowed to proceed.

The engine of this train came into contact with the engine of the down train, and, with several waggons, was also thrown off the line. Before any means could be taken remove the broken waggons, the fire from one of the engines had caught the débris, and the wind blowing through the tunnel caused the fire to spread so rapidly that it was impossible to clear the line. Arrangements were therefore made to work the traffic over the Great Eastern Railway between Hertford, Cambridge, and Peterborough, and it will continue to be so worked until the line through the tunnel is again fit for traffic.

This, it is hoped, will be the case in the course of Monday. It is hardly necessary for me to mention that the most rigid enquiry will be made as to the error of the signalman, which has had such serious results.

I am, Sir, your faithful servant,
SEYMOUR. CLARKE, General Manager.
Great Northern Railway, King's-cross Station, June 10.[6]

He was right in his hopes in one respect as, so great was the amount of incineration that had to be removed, the tunnel remained closed until 9 a.m. on Monday, but then only goods trains were allowed through; it was really Tuesday before the passenger service resumed. To everyone's relief, and probably surprise, the tunnel itself was only slightly damaged.

The two deceased excited little sympathy from the inspector, the company or the press:

Extract from Board of Trade Accident Report

The driver sent his fireman back to the guard, who was in the van at the tail of the train, to ask what he was to do.

The guard Wray looked out of the window of his van, and replied that the driver was to push the train back to the station, which, owing to the falling incline, he might have done; but the driver, very properly refused to push back the train, it being dangerous to do so, and directly contrary to the regulations of the Great Northern Railway Company. The guard Wray should have got out of his van and gone back to protect his train, but he neglected this important duty, and was killed by the first collision. Rawlins, a servant of the Metropolitan Railway Company, who had formerly been employed at New England on the Great Northern Railway, was travelling in the van with the guard. He was so severely injured, that he died on the morning of the 12th inst. His travelling in the van was contrary to the regulations of the Great Northern Railway Company.

Coroner's Court

The jury's verdict: in respect of the two signalmen 'the jury would not take on themselves the responsibility of attributing blame to either'.

Outcome

Board of Trade inspector Lt Col Rich recommended two changes to the current signalling method, which were subsequently adopted in the system of absolute block working. This meant that before a train was allowed into a section, the signalman had to positively request clearance from the next box ahead, rather than relying on the 'out of section' message for the previous train, and – a separate block telegraph that permanently displayed the state of the section was to be used, in addition to the general-purpose 'speaking' telegraph.

Glasgow Tunnel – Mission Impossible

The Shields Daily Gazette and Shipping Telegraph, **Saturday 15 December 1894**

GLASGOW TUNNEL – RESCUED UNDER GREAT DIFFICULTIES

At Glasgow this morning the woodwork of an airlock in the railway subway caught fire and 18 labouring men were entrapped in the tunnel. The fire brigade were immediately summoned, and six of the men were soon rescued, but it was found impossible to get at the others. The rescue party then entered parallel tunnel, and after breaking through the double iron tunnel, the remaining 12 men, suffering from smoke fumes were brought to the surface and sent home.

This was a subway at St Enoch Square, Glasgow, and the fire had been going on for some time. It was to be the scene of high drama – 'a mission impossible' that required all the determination of the workmen to rescue their workmates trapped inside an iron tube.

The navvies had been working in two parallels tunnels, which were being driven under the Clyde. The fire had broken out among some planking covering the iron roof of the west tunnel and smoke poured through the small spaces between the iron-casing. The men working inside the tunnel were in danger, not just from the fire but from the volume of smoke and smoke inhalation.

The rescuers had to make their way along the east tunnel and then drive through the 5ft of earth that separated the two tunnels to reach the 1in-thick iron-casing of the west tunnel. To add to their worries, it was thought that once they had broken through to the other tunnel where the fire was, the smoke would come through and overcome the rescuers.

The rescuers had managed to make an initial small opening and passed though a 1½in-diameter pipe delivering air at a pressure of 14lbs to the square inch. It was hoped that the air would keep back the smoke to a certain extent and allow the imprisoned men a certain amount of breathing space. 'They enlarged the hole to be able to also pass through a bottle of brandy ... to revive them ... and their spirits.'[7] After nine hours of arduous, heavy work they had pierced the casing using a battering ram and made a hole big enough to allow a man through. Soon after seven o' clock the next morning the rescued men were finally pulled through the hole one after the other, in just fifteen minutes.

The rescued men were thankful and more than somewhat dazed; they had all sat as near the 'air-pipe' as they could, and this had helped them a great deal, but they had been in the tunnel for seventeen hours, expecting and fearing the worse. Despite all this, many were able to walk home, although some had to be taken in cabs.

One of the rescued men, a Mr Joseph Brown, told the *Dundee Advertiser* about his experience; it sounded like an 'Indiana Jones' adventure. He said 'they had become aware of their predicament as early as 7 o'clock on the Friday night. They had tried to rush through smoke and flames but were beaten back, although some had managed to do this before the smoke increased too much (and no doubt had given the alarm). Those left made their way back up the tunnel, retreating from the smoke. None of them were 'unmanned with excitement' but they thought their best chance lay in trying to knock through to the other tunnel. Communication was kept up by the entombed men by knocking on the iron walls of the tunnel, but 11 o'clock had come and no response was heard. He thought then 'it might be all over as the smoke was fast choking them. Two or three men had been rendered senseless by the foul air and had to be dragged along.' Then brandy and air had reached them and animated their efforts; there was relief and joy at having the bottle of brandy passed through. They knew they were out of danger, although it took another six hours to be released from the tunnel.

Mission accomplished!

Cornishman, Thursday 9 May 1895
FIRE IN A TUNNEL
A fire broke out in the Glasgow subway railway on Thursday night. 40 workmen effected their escape but one was badly burnt.

Edinburgh Evening News, Thursday 5 September 1889
FIRE IN A TUNNEL
An occurrence which might have had very serious results, was fortunately discovered in good time at New Street Station, Birmingham. A driver who had just brought his engine into the station through the north tunnel reported that some of the new sleepers which had been placed in the tunnel for repairs to the permanent way were on fire. The station fire-brigade were instantly called together and proceed to the tunnel on an engine. It was found that the

sleepers had begun to blaze up fiercely and, having been creosoted they gave out an immense amount of heat and flame. The tunnel was full of smoke and the wall against which the sleepers were lying was almost red-hot. It was, therefore, with great difficulty that the fire-brigade, and the men who came to their aid, worked, and several of them were severely scorched.

Ultimately, however, the fire was got under by means of the water from the engine tank, and with the assistance of a permanent-way gang, the burning sleepers were removed.

The cutting for Severn Tunnel shows the variations in the rock strata, which caused so many different kinds of problems, particularly in respect of water and flooding. (Private collection)

FLOOD

Water was the nightmare of all who worked on tunnels, whether under river or ground. Water incapacitated workmen with ill health and exhaustion; brought contractors to their knees in trying desperately to fulfil their terms; frustrated shareholders with works being held up; and filled railway boards with fear for their companies' continued existence, as the tunnels ate up more and more money. Water costs time, money and lives.

Floods in tunnels were commonplace. The way they were dealt with called for boldness, daring and ingenuity – both in the stopping of them and in the rescuing of those trapped by the waters.

Scottish Tunnel – Drowned

Caledonian Mercury, Monday 2 December 1844

SCOTTISH TUNNEL – DROWNED

An occurrence of a most alarming and unfortunately fatal nature occurred on Friday morning in the drift-way of the tunnel now forming for the Edinburgh and Leith Railway, by which the works have been much damaged and four lives lost.

Our readers are aware that the chief feature in this line of railway is a tunnel through the whole extent of the New

Town, from Canal Street on the south to Canonmills on the north. The tunnel runs across Prince's Street, through St Andrew Square, down Duke Street and Dublin Street, through Drummond Place, and down Scotland Street, in the low ground at Canonmills, where it again emerges into the open air. The making of this extensive tunnel had been divided into three or four contracts, and the drift-way of them all had been nearly completed; the last being the centre one, where the melancholy accident occurred, extending from about the foot of Duke Street to a considerable way down Dublin Street. The cause of this boring being left was in consequence of an interdict from Government, which obliged the contractors to work the drift from the upper end. This drift-way, it may be necessary to explain, is a comparatively small shaft bored through the ground, and being afterwards widened and lengthened,

A flooded Queensbury Tunnel gives the feel of what it would have been like battling flooding waters. The tranquillity belies the reality of what would have been rising waters full of mud, sand, rubble and debris, and the real possibility of drowning for the men. (Courtesy of Phill Davison)

forms the completed tunnel. The drift-way in this railway, we understand, was so high that a man could walk upright, but not very broad.

That portion of the line extending through St Andrew Square has long been completed, and has been standing unused and unworked for the last seven or eight months, and during all that time there has been a gradual accumulation of water in the mine, being fed from the springs of the old North Loch and other water courses in the bowels of the earth in that direction. Of this the contractors were well aware. As the miners, however, were gradually carrying the drift-way in the centre contract up Duke Street to meet it, and were coming near to the point of junction between the two, they felt the necessity of proceeding with caution, so that the pent-up waters in the upper drift might find a vent through the nearly opened shaft without injuring the works or endangering life. Why this course, obviously, so full of hazard, was adopted, rather than the more safe one of pumping the water to the surface, does not appear, unless it may be inferred that the additional expense this would entail upon the works deterred them. If so, this is one added to many melancholy instances which might be adduced, of a narrow economy, in the first instance not only causing many valuable lives to be sacrificed, but of adding in the end, tenfold to the expense of the operation.

The works were carried on day and night, and the workmen, three or four of whom could only get to the place at once, were employed in three divisions, working eight hours each, and descending by the shaft or eye sunk at the head of Dublin Street. As they had been for some days in expectation of meeting with the water by penetrating to the other shaft, the attention of all was naturally called to every symptom of the gushing of water. On Thursday, one of the workmen was working on the west side of the drift, when four or five small jets of water gushed out. He called the attention of his companions to the circumstance, who thought it was the pent up flood, and, throwing down their tools, were about to run for safety; but the man who first discovered it assured them it was a small spring in the place; and on the jets stopping a short time after, they began to be reassured. There was another workman who had been employed in the upper mine that mentioned to his companions he thought they had deviated from the line of the other shaft, but no attention was paid to his remarks. On Thursday night, however, Mr Mitchell, the contractor, becoming anxious about the joining, gave directions that when the morning shift of men went down at six o'clock, he should be called as he meant to go down with them and ascertain the progress they had made. Accordingly, on Friday morning, Erskine, the ganger or superintendent of the men, was to have called on Mr Mitchell, but for some reason or other he did not do so, but he spoke to his brother, Mr Peter Mitchell, a person who was employed by his brother to superintend the workmen generally, but who was not conversant with the business of mining. He was induced to go down with Erskine, about six in the morning, where two men were already working.

What passed in the mine after this can only be a matter of conjecture. But a short time after Mr Mitchell and the ganger had gone down, about half-past six, a boy, about fourteen years of age, named Jack, was lowered down the shaft, when at the bottom, and before he had let go his hold of the rope by which he had descended, he heard a noise, as he describes it: 'like a loud roar of thunder' at the head of the drift. Terrified with the sound and instantly divining the cause, he cried to the men above to hoist him up. They also had heard the noise, and animated by the same terrors, they drew him quickly to the surface. Scarcely had he reached it, when a huge wave came surging up the shaft, a perpendicular height of eighty feet, the spray from which dashed fiercely against the roof of the wooden shed that encloses the descent. But this was only for an instant.

Falling back again into the shaft, almost as quickly as it had risen, the angry waters began to find a vent through the drift which leads from the shaft down Dublin Street. The opening that had been made, however, was altogether inadequate to afford a channel to the torrent, so long pent up; and besides the debris brought down from the sides of the drift began to choke up the passage, and again to dam up the course of the torrent. In consequence of this, and the great compression of air in the mine, a second explosion took place at the foot of Dublin Street, this time towards the surface, when the water poured out upon the street, nearly opposite the entrance to the Broughton Markets, to such an extent that the area of Mr Brace, spirit dealer in Dublin Street, was flooded to the extent of about four feet, while a considerable volume poured down into Drummond Place. But the main stream continued its course underground, to the entrance of the drift at Canonmills, where it flooded the terminus of the completed portion of the railway to a considerable extent, filling up, for a time, the whole breadth of the railway line.

So soon as the workmen on the surface had recovered from the surprise and fright this sudden bursting had caused among them, their first thought was for the four unhappy men who were down in the mine. That they could have survived such an enormous rush of water was impossible; the most sanguine could not entertain a hope of their escape. Nevertheless, as soon as the water had subsided in the shaft, men went down, and after some little search they succeeded in finding the bodies of Erskine, the ganger, and of Blair, a miner from Liberton, which were lying at the bottom of the shaft. They were, as might be expected, quite dead; and appeared to have been swept down from the point of bursting to the place where they were found, and there to have been caught in the eddy caused by the circular shaft. The others were not then to be found, and it was supposed had been swept down the drift-way.

The noise occasioned by the bursting of the waters was distinctly heard by the families in the street; and the news of the melancholy accident having soon spread, a crowd was quickly collected, which continued about the works the whole day. Information being conveyed to the Police Office, a force was speedily despatched to the spot who rendered great service in keeping off the crowd, and otherwise preserving order. We may mention, also, that in the course of the forenoon, Bailie Mack, Mr Dymock, the procurator-fiscal, and Mr Haining, the superintendent of police, visited the scene of the accident, examined the workmen as to its origin, and otherwise took all the necessary steps to obtain judicial and precise information in regard to it.

The fate of the two miners, whose names are Blair and Philips, is invested with a melancholy interest. We have already mentioned that the work was carried on night and day; and these men had gone down at ten o'clock on the previous night, and should have been released at six o'clock on Friday morning. Owing, however, to the fact that the men who should have relieved them had slept longer than usual, they continued to work and were thus involved in the dreadful calamity. Indeed, at so critical a period did the accident happen, that the relieving men had arrived at the shed and engaged in putting on their working-dress to descend into the mine, when they were alarmed by the crash of the eruption. The poor boy, too, we have mentioned, had a narrow escape. A few minutes longer, a few yards farther advanced into the mine, and no human power could have saved him. He seemed to be duly sensible of his perilous escape; and the wild expression of alarm pictured on his countenance hours after the accident, testified to the vivid impression made on him by the danger. Erskine, the ganger, had gone down just before him, and could not have reached the place where the men were working when the eruption took place. The boy states that he was only a few yards up the drift, and that he heard him utter a loud shriek at the

time of the crash, as if he also then had become aware of
his awfully perilous situation. We may mention that all
the four unfortunate men were married and had families.
The wife of one of them, Philips, whose body had not
been recovered, resorted to the scene in the course of the
forenoon, and her wild shrieks and cries were calculated to
touch the coldest heart.

The water continued to flow at the aperture in Canonmills
during the whole of the day, and the mine remained with
from four to five feet depth of water in it during the greater
part of the day. The slowness of its progress at last, compared
with its fury on its first eruption, may be accounted for
by the fact that debris brought down by the torrent had
filled the narrow passage – and particularly at the bottom
of Dublin Street, where the water forced its way to the
surface, the drift had partially fallen in, the level of the street
having perceptibly fallen. There is also on the north side
of Drummond Place a ridge of rock intersecting the drift,
through which a passage is drilled, but so small as to prevent
the great torrent of water forcing its way at once. Owing
to these impediments, the water could only be drained off
gradually. At the Canonmills station a channel was cut for
the stream, conducting it into a common sewer on the line
of railway, which carried it off.

All the bodies were recovered. *Erskine* and *Blair*, as we
have mentioned, were discovered about half-past ten in
the forenoon at the bottom of the shaft. They were found
together, Blair's hand grasping the leg of Erskine – a position
which would indicate that Blair had sought safety in flight
down the drift, and had reached Erskine, but were both
overtaken by the raging flood, which no speed could have
outstripped. The bodies of *Philips* and *Mitchell* were found,
the former about three, the latter about four o'clock in the
afternoon. They had been carried down the mine as far as
to the rocky ridge we have mentioned below Drummond
Place, where their farther progress was stayed by this

barrier. They were brought to the surface in the presence of a collected crowd, and Philip's wife, who could not be long kept away from the scene of the calamity, renewed her lamentations at the sight of her husband's corpse.

We need not add that this melancholy event formed the theme of conversation in the city, or that it has spread a general gloom over the workmen engaged in these operations. The deceased were all respected by their companions. Erskine was a faithful and vigilant superintendent, and the loss of Mr Mitchell, the brother of the master, is deeply regretted by the men. He was employed as general superintendent of the contract, and had the happy art of gaining the good will of those under him without neglecting the interests of his employers. As the families of all these poor men, with the exception, perhaps, of Mitchell are left destitute, a public subscription for their behalf will be necessary, unless, indeed, the directors of the railway follow the laudable example of the Marquis of Londonderry – an example not more laudable than it appears to be just – who makes it a point of providing from his own funds for the families of all the workmen who have the misfortune to lose their lives in his coal mines.

Severn Tunnel – Enough for a Lifetime

Sub-aqueous tunnels have recently become quite the fashion. One such experience as the Severn Tunnel with its ever-varying and strangely contorted strata, and the dangers from floods above and floods below has been sufficient for me. One sub-aqueous tunnels is quite enough for a life-time.

(Thomas A. Walker, sub-contractor who worked at the tunnel 1880–87)

The tunnel – 4 miles and 28½ chains (7,668 yards, as identified on the completed plan) under the River Severn and adjacent

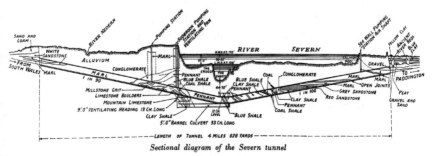

Sectional diagram of the Severn tunnel

Diagram of Severn Tunnel. (Private collection)

Severn Tunnel's lead diver Alexander Lambert – here in the bowler hat attending a diving exhibition – was a very special man. He did not directly save lives but, nonetheless, was a hero. He boldly went where other men dared not go, and solved problems they could not. He later became a lead marine diver with Siebe Gorman's company and gained a reputation as a shark fighter in the Indian Ocean. *Un homme extraordinaire!* (Private collection)

ground – was the preferred option of the Great Western Railway Company, as opposed to a bridge, to give a direct route into Wales. If they had known of the battle that lay ahead of them, perhaps they would have chosen differently. When Frederick A. Talbot wrote his book, *Railway Wonders of the World* (1913), he included the Severn Tunnel as one of the wonders. Jack Hayward (2015) goes even further declaring, 'If ever there is to be an eighth wonder of the world then it should be none other than the Severn Tunnel.'[1] It is truly remarkable that it was ever achieved. It was to be a battle of epic proportions – man against nature for fourteen hard, soul-destroying years, until modern technology tamed the beast known as the Great Spring!

Whilst always associated with the Great Western Railway Company – especially Sir Daniel Gooch and Sir John Hawkshaw – the Severn Tunnel was actually the brainchild of Charles Richardson. He planned, appealed Parliament (with the GWR) and worked on the tunnel for the first seven years. Richardson was an eminent civil engineer of his day having served his apprenticeship with Isambard Kingdom Brunel in 1833. He had been baptised in the art of tunnelling while working under Sir Marc Brunel, Isambard's father, on the Thames Tunnel.[2] Sadly, after his seven-year struggle, the GWR lost faith in Richardson's ability to deliver, and placed him under Sir John Hawkshaw.

Started in 1873, it was all progressing very slowly, when in October 1879, after six years' work it had just five shafts and a small heading, Sir Daniel Gooch invited guests to visit the beginnings of the tunnel. He joked, 'It will be rather wet, you had better bring your umbrellas,' but had no idea just how wet this job would turn out to be.[3] Tides and springs, spring tides and the Great Spring, would flood the shafts, the headings, the tunnel, again and again, causing collapse, destruction and loss of life. So often did this happen that a number of divers were employed to go down into the deep, murky floods to try to find and remedy the problems. The tides in the Severn Estuary stand third in the list of the highest tides in the world, with a rise of 31.5ft (9.6m). One reason for this is the funnel-like shape of the estuary with its steady decrease causing the volume to rise – up to 50ft in places along its route. Whilst everyone had expected danger in tunnelling under such a river, little had they anticipated the more real danger of tunnelling under the land with its rich supply of subterranean water sources. At one time almost every well, spring and little river for almost 5 miles between Sudbrook Camp and Portskewett village poured itself into the tunnel until it ran dry. The village was empty of water, but the tunnel was full! [4]

Taking One's Life in One's Breathing Apparatus
On 16 October 1879, when the Great Spring burst through Richardson's heading at Sudbrook, all work was brought to a standstill. It would take fourteen tiresome, dangerous months to bring the spring under control, so work could begin again. At this time it was sub-contractor Thomas Walker, an engineer of high standing, who had to deal with the management and solve the problem. Enter stage right, or rather down the shaft, one Alexander Lambert, diver, and man of 'extraordinary courage'.[5] His job sounds simple – to shut the flood door – but to do it he had to descend 130ft in the murky, flooded Sudbrook Old Shaft, grope his way 340 yards forward along the heading in the utter darkness, negotiating the broken timbers, general debris and rubble washed down by the flood, somehow remove the laid rails and cross-sleepers on the ground, and then shut the flood door. Not a job for the faint-hearted. It was no easy task even if one already knew the layout and the way, but Lambert had never been there before. It is hard to imagine the nerves of steel, true grit and determination that one man had to possess to fulfil this job, but Lambert showed he had them by the bucket load.[6]

Wearing his usual diving suit with its 60lbs metal helmet and attached air pipe, 40lbs iron breastplate and heavy boots, he made his first attempt. Carrying a short iron bar, he entered the heading stumbling over debris; in complete darkness he inched forward feeling his way through broken timbers and supports. Struggling against a strong current, the air pipe attached to his helmet floated along the roof of the heading, but soon his strength began to fail and he was unable to drag it along further than 270 yards. He was forced to turn back when he was within 70 yards of the door; and it was while retracing his steps that he found himself in serious trouble. When he reached the double-timbered heading, his air pipe curled up in kinks and coiled around the timbers of the headings. Working alone and in complete darkness, he had to untangle his air pipe and carry these coils, which constantly slipped from his grasp, all the while knowing everything depended on the safety of his air pipe, without which he would not come out alive.[7]

Walker was also a man determined to succeed; his reputation was on the line, so he cast around for a better piece of equipment to enable his divers to conclude the work.

Henry Albert Fleuss was experimenting with his invention of a new diving suit incorporating its own rebreathing equipment, which required no air-feed pipes but was carried on the diver's back. It was the first self-contained underwater breathing apparatus (scuba): 'The suit was made of a rubberised material whilst under the helmet one wore a facemask connected by two breathing tubes to a copper tank filled with compressed oxygen (not air) and a carbon dioxide absorbent material that allowed the same oxygen to be used for three hours.'[8] Fleuss agreed to Walker's invitation to come and try out the untested suit in a real-life situation, and to complete the necessary task. Fleuss was, at this time, an inexperienced diver and had only tested the suit in a water tank.

On 3 November 1880 history was made. When Fleuss arrived on site, he was shown drawings of the tunnel workings. Wearing the new suit, he would be accompanied by Lambert wearing his old suit with its air pipe. They descended the shaft, with Lambert in the lead as guide, and entered the heading, moving forward on hands and knees following the rails for a quarter of a mile. They had worked through a tangled mass of debris and fallen rock before Fleuss lost his nerve and they returned to the surface. He told Walker that he would not go down there again for £10,000.[9]

Fleuss did, however, reluctantly agree to allow the willing Lambert to use his equipment in another attempt. Once inside the new suit and after a quick course of instruction, Lambert descended yet again, but an hour and a half later he returned to the surface; he had reached the door but only managed to lift one rail and close one of the valves. One further, desperate, attempt and Lambert had successfully closed the door, removed the second rail and, he believed, closed both valves. Still all was not well as the water continued to pour in. Back he had to go again, when, to his horror, he found that 'instead of closing the valves he had opened them wide so that as fast as the water was being pumped out, it was flooding in through the valves; he had failed to understand that the valves had left-hand threads and needed to be closed in the opposite direction to what he had supposed on his first attempt'.[10] He made good his mistake and soon work could start again.

The Fleuss suit was a game changer for diving – the first 'rebreather'; the first 'self-contained underwater breathing apparatus' (scuba). It was the point in diving history that would eventually lead to the scuba diving we know today. Still difficult, heavy and cumbersome, it was a vast improvement in manoeuvrability over the previous air-tube-fed system. It made man free to roam underwater. (Private collection)

Rescue! How happy the trapped men would have been to see this lifeboat arriving, saving them from probable death as most would not have been able to swim to safety, even though their lives would have depended on it. (Private collection)

What is incredible in all of this is that, despite the high level of danger, increased further by using an untried new invention, no lives were lost.

Trapped

At 7 p.m. on 17 October 1883 a night shift of ninety men descended into Marsh Pit for their usual toil. What was to become a 'perfect storm' was blowing. It was known that one of the highest tides of the year would occur that night – but not one this high. Suddenly a great tidal wave, some 5–6ft high, burst over the whole low-lying ground between the river and the shaft, flooding the whole of the place in several feet of water. Passing beyond the houses, it reached the boilers that worked the winding and pumping engines at the shaft, extinguishing the fires (making them inoperable) and then poured down into the pit with a fall of 100ft – it was a mighty waterfall. Luckily there was a ladder-way up the side of the shaft and some men had made their escape up this and given the alarm. One less fortunate making his way up was knocked off the ladder by the force of the water, thrown back and drowned. That left eighty-three men and boys trapped at the bottom of the shaft with rising water (the gradient in the tunnel here was 1 in 90 to the west).

At the top of the shaft the men who had managed to make their way there through the floodwaters tried to stem the downward flow by building a dam of anything they could find – clothing, sacks, timber, anything to hand. Despite their efforts the water in the tunnel continued rising to within 8ft of the crown of the arch. Eventually the tide gradually retreated and the dam at the top began to be more effective; thoughts then turned to how to rescue the men trapped in the darkness below. These men had retreated as high as was possible and sat not knowing the extent of the flooding, not knowing how long the air would last, not knowing their fate. Up on top a boat was brought and lowered, with a few brave men with lights, down into the unknown. Just a short distance into the tunnel the men found their way was blocked by stout timbers, forcing them back to the shaft where they obtained a crow-saw to enable them to cut through the obstacles. The work was hard and slow – and then they dropped the saw into the water. They had to go back and sit and wait for another to arrive in order to start again. Eventually they broke through. Slowly, a few at a time, the trapped men were rescued. By the morning of 18 October all were safe and accounted for.

Whilst all was well with the workforce, the works was in the worst position it had been in since January 1881. Yet again Diver Lambert's services were called into action, and, once again, he did the job.

Bibliograpy

PRIMARY SOURCES

Board of Trade railway accident reports

Newspapers

Belfast Commercial Chronicle

Cambridge Independent Press

Cheltenham Chronicle

Dorset Chronicle and Somersetshire
Chronicle

Dundee Advertiser

Evening Mail

Hampshire

Hampshire Telegraph and Sussex
Chronicle

Leeds Times

Leicester Chronicle and Leicestershire
Mercury

London Evening Standard

Morning Advertiser

Newry Telegraph

Reading Mercury

Reynolds Newspapers

The Belfast News

The Bristol Mercury

The Courier

The Derby Mercury

The Hampshire Advertiser

The Huddersfield Chronicle and
Yorkshire Advertiser

The Ipswich Journal

The Liverpool Mercury

The Luton Times and Dunstable
Herald

The Morning Post

The Standard

The Taunton Courier

The Times

The Western Daily Press

York Herald

Magazines

Bell's Weekly Messenger

Freeman's Journal

Oxford Journal

The Grantham Journal

The Spectator

The Railway Magazine

Worcester Journal

SECONDARY SOURCES

Books

Bagwell, Phillip S., *The Railway-Men: The History of the National Union of Railwaymen*. George Allan & Unwin Ltd, 1963.

Brees, S.C., *Appendix to Railway Practice* … J.Williams, 1839.

Burton, Anthony, *The Railway Builders*. John Murray, 1992.

Chapman, W.G., *Track Topics: A Book of Railway Engineering for Boys of All Ages*. David & Charles, reprint 1971 (first published by GWR, 1935).

Coleman, Terry, *The Railway Navvies: A History of the Men who Made the Railways*. Hutchinson of London, 1965.

Drake, James, *Road Book of the London and Birmingham Railway*. Hayward and Moore, 1839.

Freeling, Arthur, *The Railway Companion: From London to Birmingham*. Whittaker & Co., 1839.

Joby, R.S., *The Railway Builders: Lives and Works of Victorian Railway Builders*. David & Charles, 1983.

Macdermot, E.T., *History of the Great Western Railway: Vol. I, Part I and II 1833–1863* and *Vol. II 1863–1921*. Great Western Railway Company, 1927.

Matheson, Rosa, *Death, Dynamite and Disaster: A Grisly British Railway History*. The History Press, 2014.

Morgan, Bryan (ed.), *The Railway-Lover's Companion*. Eyre & Spottiswoode Ltd, 1963.

Pendleton, John, *Our Railways: Their Origin, Development, Incident and Romance, Vol. 11*. Cassell & Co., 1894.

Rolt, L.T.C., *Red For Danger: A History of Railway Accidents and Railway Safety*. Fourth Edition, David & Charles, 1982.

Schieldrop, Edgar B., *Conquest of Space and Time: The Railway*. Hutchinson & Co. Publishers Ltd, English Version, 1939.

Searle, Muriel V., *Down the Line to Brighton*. Baton Transport, 1986.

Simmons, Jack (ed.), *The Railway Traveller's Handy Book*. Adam & Dart, 1972 (first published 1862).

Talbot, Frederick A., *Railway Wonders of the World*. Cassell & Co., 1913.

Vaughan, Adrian, *Isambard Kingdom Brunel: Engineering Knight-Errant*. John Murray, 1991.

Walker, Thomas A., *The Severn Tunnel: Its Construction and Difficulties 1872–1887*. Richard Bentley & Sons, 1888.

Journals, Papers and Talks

Beynon, Meurig, 'Empirical Modelling and the Foundations of Artificial Intelligence'. Department of Computer Science, University of Warwick.

Davy, C., 'The Kilsby Tunnel: Birmingham Railway', in *Mechanics' Magazine, Museum, Register, Journal, and Gazette*. Vol. 28 (7 October 1837–31 March 1838), pp. 210–11.

Hayward, Jack, 'The Severn Tunnel' (in four parts), in *STEAM Magazine*, 2015.

The Household Narrative of Current Events, 1851.

Porter, David, 'Persistent Analogue Threats: Fallible Humans and Resonating Systems'. RSA Security Conference, London, June 2015.

Preece, William Henry, MICE, 'On Railway Telegraphs'. Before the Institution of Civil Engineers, January 1863.

Schmidt, Dr Felix, 'Genius or Great Systems Engineers: Isambard Kingdon Brunel'. Civil Engineering, University of Birmingham, at INCOSE at Network Rail, June 2007.

Slater, Dr David, 'Cambrensis: The Clayton Tunnel Case Study'. An iDEPEND/FRAM test case, 2013.

Timbs, J. 'The London & Birmingham Railway', in *The Literary World: A Journal of Popular Information and Entertainment*. No. 13 (22 June 1839), pp. 193–6.

Wilmot, George, 'The Railway in Finchley: A Study in Suburban Development'. Library and Arts Committee, LBB, 1973.

Websites

archive.org/details/drakesroadbookof00drak – James Drake, *Road Book of the London and Birmingham Railway*, 1825.

archive.org/stream/ – George F. Chambers, *Eastbourne Memories of the Victorian Period 1845–1901 and Some Other Things of Interest – Divers and Sundry*.

booksnow1.scholarsportal.info/ebooks/oca2/22/historyofgreatno00grinuoft/historyofgreatno00grinuoft.pdf –

Charles H. Grinling, 'The History of the Great Northern Railway 1845–1895', Methuen & Co., 1898.

gerald-massey.org.uk/Railway/c07_construction_(I.).htm – Francis Fox MInstCE, 'River, Road, and Rail: Some Engineering Reminiscences', 1904.

history.wiltshire.gov.uk/community/getcom2.php?id=24

onlinebooks.library.upenn.edu/webbin/book/lookupname?key=Brees%2C%20S.%20C.%20(Samuel%20Charles) – 'The Online Books Page Writings of Samuel Charles Brees, Civil Engineer'.

thebeautyoftransport.wordpress.com – Daniel Wright, 'The Beauty of Transport' blog.

wondersofworldengineering.com/severn-tunnel.html – 'Conquest of the Severn', July 1937.

www.arct.cam.ac.uk/Downloads/chs/vol5/article3.pdf – David Brooke, 'The Railway Navvy: A Reassessment', *Construction History Vol. 5*, 1989.

www.bristol.ac.uk/library/resources/specialcollections/archives/brunel/ikblockeddiary.pdf – 'The Personal Journal of I.K. Brunel', introductory note and annotations by R. Angus Buchanan, 2011

www.cs.indiana.edu/classes/p415-sjoh/readings/ClaytonTunnel/ – Gerard J. Holzmann, 'Clayton Tunnel Disaster', in *Design and Validation of Computer Protocols*. Prentice Hall Software Series and AT&T Bell Telephone Laboratories, 1991.

www.djo.org.uk/household-words.html – H.J. Brown, 'Navvies as They Used to Be', *Household Words*. Vol. XIII, No. 3621 (January 1856).

www.engineering-timelines.com/scripts/engineeringItems –

www.forgottenrelics.co.uk/tunnels/construction/overview.html – Stephen Prior, 'The Victorian Art of Tunnel Construction'.

www.queensburytunnel.org.uk/history/overview.shtml – Queensbury Tunnel Society.

www.watfordobserver.co.uk/news/14558133.Nostalgia__The_tunnel_disaster_that_shook_Watford/ – Kelly Pells, 'The Tunnel Disaster that Shook Watford', *Watford Observer*, 2016.

Notes

INTRODUCTION

1   *Aberdeen Evening Express*, 1 April 1886.
2   David John Pollard, tunnel researcher.
3   Schieldrop, *Conquest of Space and Time*.
4   Drake, *Road Book of the London & Birmingham Railway*.
5   *Liverpool Mercury*, 5 September 1828.
6   www.butterleygangroad.co.uk.
7   http://en.wikipedia.org/wiki/Tunnel.
8   Ibid.
9   Ibid.
10 Ibid.
11 Ibid.
12 Ibid.
13 Homer's land of perpetual fog and darkness.
14 Drake, op. cit.
15 Simmons (ed.), *The Railway Traveller's Handy Book*.
16 Ibid.
17 John Francis, 'The Navigator', in Morgan, *The Railway-Lover's Companion*.
18 Brown, 'Navvies as They Used to Be', in *Household Words*, Vol. XIII, No. 3621.

Chapter 1

ACCIDENTS

1   These newspaper cutting quotes courtesy of Doreen Lindegard
     from Bristol Family History Society.
2   *Bradford Observer*, 5 November 1874.
3   *Leeds Times*, 7 November 1874; www.forgottenrelics.co.uk/tunnels.
4   *Bradford Observer*, 11 November 1874.
5   Thanks to David Porter for this quote from his paper, 'Persistent
     analogue threats: fallible humans and resonating systems', RSA
     Security Conference, London, June 2015.
6   Matheson, *Death Dynamite and Disaster.*
7   *Morning Post*, Tuesday 19 June 1849.
8   *The Bradford Observer*, 21 June 1849.
9   Otley Town Council information sheet.
10   Hopefully that will all change if the current restoration project as
     a cycleway is achieved.
11   This analogy has been borrowed from the work of Arthur
     Freeling writing on the Great Kilsby Tunnel.
12   www.queensburytunnel.org.uk.
13   www.28dayslater.co.uk/queensbury-tunnel-history-and-big-pics.
     t13949.
14   www.queensburytunnel.org.uk/history/overview.shtml.
15   All newspaper cuttings on Queensbury Tunnel provided by www.
     forgottenrelics.co.uk.
16   www.pendonmuseum.com/audio/railway-workers.
17   NUR MSS.127/AS/4/1 – *The Railway Review*, 1881, p.10.
18   *Cheltenham Chronicle*, 18 April 1896.
19   *Tamworth Herald*, 18 April 1896.
20   *South Wales Daily News*, 17 April 1896.

Chapter 2

COLLAPSE

1   *The Spectator*, September 1854.
2   www.victorianweb.org.
3   gerald-massey.org.uk/Railway/c07_construction_(I.).htm –
    *Notes and Extracts on the History of the London & Birmingham
    Railway*, 6 May 1833.
4   Roscoe and Lecount, *The London and Birmingham Railway*,
    Charles Tilt, 1839.
5   My italics.
6   Freeling, *The Railway Companion*.
7   Brown, op. cit., pp.543–50.
8   www.forgottenrelics.co.uk/tunnels/construction/overview.html.
9   Brown, op. cit.
10 *The Buckinghamshire Herald*, 25 July 1835.
11 Ibid., 22 August 1835.
12 Ibid.
13 *Morning Post*, 17 August 1835.
14 Information taken from *Morning Advertiser*, 20 August 1835.
15 Fox, *River, Road, and Rail*.
16 Brees, S.C. (Samuel Charles), 1839, p.18.
17 *Morning Post*, 4 April 1842.
18 Ibid.
19 *Cambridge Independent Press*, 16 April 1842.
20 *The Standard*, 4 April 1842.
21 *Morning Post*, 4 April 1842; *The Chronicle*, 6 April 1842.
22 *Morning Post*, 4 April 1842.
23 Ibid.
24 *The Spectator*, 30 September 1854.
25 *Newry Telegraph*, 26 September 1854.
26 *Wiltshire Independent*, 28 September 1854.
27 *Leeds Times*, 23 September 1854.

Chapter 3

COLLISIONS

1   Porter, 'Persistent Analogue Threats'.
2   www.pendonmuseum.com/audio/railway-workers.
3   Charles G. Harper, *The Brighton Road*. Cecil Palmer, 1922.
4   Preece, 'On Railway Telegraphs'.
5   Slater, 'Cambrensis: The Clayton Tunnel Case Study'.
6   Board of Trade Report.
7   *Brighton Gazette*, 29 August 1861.
8   *Liverpool Daily Post*, 26 August 1861.
9   *Brighton Gazette*, 29 August 1861.
10   Ibid.
11   Ibid., 29 August 1861.
12   *Bell's Weekly Messenger*, 16 September 1861.
13   Chambers, George F., *Eastbourne Memories*.
14   Porter, op. cit.
15   Quotes taken from *Reynolds Newspaper*, 18 December 1864.
16   *The Belfast News*, 22 December 1864.
17   *The Standard*, 18 January 1865.
18   Extracts from *London Evening Standard*, 4 January 1865.
19   George Wilmot, 'The Railway in Finchley: A Study in Suburban Development'. Library and Arts Committee, LBB, 1973.
20   *London Daily News*, 12 December 1881.
21   *Leicester Chronicle*, 18 November 1882.
22   *York Herald*, 4 May 1884.
23   *Worcester Journal*, 7 January 1882.

Chapter 4

EXPLOSIONS

1   Walker, *The Severn Tunnel*.
2   Ibid.

3   Ibid.
4   All quotes for this piece taken from *Bristol Mercury*, 1 January 1842.
5   Ibid., 29 January 1842.
6   Major A. Ford RA, HM's Inspector of Explosives Report.
7   Ibid.
8   *The Grantham Journal*, Saturday 16 December 1876.
9   Ford, HM's Inspector of Explosives Report.
10   Matheson, op. cit.
11   *The Western Daily Express*, 30 September 1879.
12   Read *Death, Dynamite and Disaster* to see how he became the first bomb disposal man.
13   *Hampshire Telegraph and Sussex Chronicle*, 26 April 1876.
14   Majendie was heavily involved in the 'The Dynamite Wars' with the Fenians – see *Death Dynamite and Disaster*.
15   www.forgottenrelics.co.uk/accidentaldeath/cymmer.html.

Chapter 5

FIRE

1   Charles H. Grinling, *The History of the Great Northern Railway 1845–1895*.
2   Ibid.
3   *The Times*, Monday 11 June 1866.
4   Ibid.
5   Gringling.
6   Information source: Lawson Thompson Scrapbooks, Hitchin Museum – www.geograph.org.uk.
7   *Dundee Advertiser*, Monday 17 December 1894.

Chapter 6

FLOODS

1   Jack Hayward, 'The Severn Tunnel' (in 4 parts), Friends of *STEAM Magazine*, 2015.

2   Ibid.

3   Walker, op. cit.

4   Ibid.

5   Hayward, op. cit.

6   Read of another such intrepid diver, Harry Watts, who worked on recovery in the Tay Bridge Disaster in *Death, Dynamite and Disaster*.

7   Hayward, op. cit.

8   Ibid.

9   Ibid.

10   Ibid.